G000077178

The Em@il Joke Book

FIRST PUBLISHED IN GREAT BRITAIN IN 2009 BY PRION
AN IMPRINT OF THE
CARLTON PUBLISHING GROUP
20 MORTIMER STREET
LONDON W1T 3JW

10 9 8 7 6 5 4 3 2 1

COPYRIGHT © 2009 CARLTON PUBLISHING GROUP

ALL RIGHTS RESERVED. THIS BOOK IS SOLD SUBJECT TO
THE CONDITION THAT IT MAY NOT BE REPRODUCED, STORED
IN A RETRIEVAL SYSTEM OR TRANSMITTED IN ANY FORM
OR BY MEANS, ELECTRONIC, MECHANICAL, PHOTOCOPYING,
RECORDING OR OTHERWISE, WITHOUT THE PUBLISHER'S PRIOR
CONSENT.

AUTHOR'S ACKNOWLEDGEMENT
HUW JARSZ WOULD LIKE TO THANK THE FOLLOWING, WITHOUT
WHOM THIS BOOK WOULD NOT BE NEARLY AS BIG, OR FUNNY:

BELINDA ANDERSON, EMMA BAILEY, STEVE BEHAN, DAVID
BOWMAN, CLARE BAGGALEY, NICK BAKER, CELINE BALL,
LUCY COLEY, VANESSA DAUBNEY, CHRISTOPHE DILLINGER,
CAROLINE FAUCHET, KARIN FREMER, LISA FRENCH, MIRANDA
FILBEE, JIM GREENHOUGH, ROLAND HALL, MICHELE HIRST,
GILLIAN HOLMES, NICK JOHNSTON, SIMON KINGSLEY, GARRY
LEWIS, STEPHANIE MCCARTHY, JOHN MAYNARD, JUDITH MOORE,
PIERS MURRAY HILL, EMMA NORLEDGE, PUG, PUGZMATE, JIM
RENNIE, LORNA RUSSELL, JEREMY SOUTHGATE, CHRISTINA
SOUTHGATE, CRAIG STEVENS, PENNY STOCK, ALISON TUTTON,
ADAM WRIGHT, EMMA YEXLEY.

A CATALOGUE RECORD FOR THIS BOOK IS AVAILABLE FROM
THE BRITISH LIBRARY

ISBN 978-1-85375-714-3

PRINTED IN CHINA

SOME OF THE TEXT IN THIS BOOK PREVIOUSLY APPEARED IN
SUBJECT: HUMOUR

The
Em@il
Joke Book

FWD @ YOUR PERIL

Compiled by Huw Jarsz

PRION

INTRODUCTION

PEOPLE OFTEN SAY TO ME HUW, WHERE DID YOU GET THAT GREAT JOKE? AND WHEN I TELL THEM IT WAS IN AN EMAIL THEY JUST DON'T BELIEVE ME. THEY THINK MY JOKES ARE MUCH TOO FUNNY TO HAVE APPEARED, AS IF BY WIRELESS MAGIC, IN MY INBOX. BUT I HAVE SPENT YEARS, TO MIX A METAPHOR, SORTING THROUGH MY INBOX CHAFF AND SELECTING, TRIMMING AND NURTURING THE BEAUTIFUL BLOOMS WHILE DISCARDING THE DRIBBLING SLOP LIKE SO MUCH USED JET-TRASH. THE BOOK YOU HOLD IN YOUR HANDS IS THE FINELY FILTERED REMAINS OF A MILLION BYTES OF FUNNY STORIES AND MULTI-MEGAPIXELS-WORTH OF ONE-LINERS. AND VERY FUNNY IT IS TOO.

DO, HOWEVER, REMEMBER THAT THIS IS A BOOK FOR GROWN-UPS AND THAT MANY OF THE JOKES HAVE NAUGHTY FOUR-LETTER WORDS IN THEM, AND I DON'T MEAN 'WILD'. I MEAN SWEAR WORDS AND ADULT THEMES LIKE SEX, VIOLENCE, AND, UM, SEXY VIOLENCE. OH, AND POO. I THINK IT'S ALL FUNNY WHEN DIRECTED TO THE RIGHT PEOPLE – ADULTS. IT'S A BIT LIKE WHEN PEOPLE COMMENT ON MY NAME. AS I SAY TO THEM, "IT IS BIG AND IT IS CLEVER!"

HUW JARSZ, LONDON 2009

TWO PRAYERS.

WOMAN'S POEM:
Before I lay me down to sleep
I pray for a man who's not a creep,
One who's handsome, smart and strong,
One who loves to listen long,
One who thinks before he speaks,
One who'll call, not wait for weeks.
I pray he's gainfully employed,
And when I spend is not annoyed.
Pulls out my chair, opens my door,
Massages my back and begs for more.
Oh send me a man who'll make love to my mind,
Who knows what to say to "How big's my behind?"
I pray that this man will love me to the end,
And always be my very best friend.

MAN'S POEM:
I pray for a mute, nymphomaniac gymnast with huge boobs who owns a bar on a golf course and loves to send me fishing and drinking. This doesn't rhyme or scan, and I don't give a shit.

SORTED WITH THE MISSUS

Just after I got married, I was invited out for a night with the boys. I told my wife that I would be home by midnight... promise! Well, the hours passed and the beer was going down way too easy. At around 3a.m. drunk as a skunk, I headed for home. Just as I got in the door, the cuckoo clock in the hall started up, and cuckooed three times. Quickly I realized she'd probably wake up, so I cuckooed another nine times. I was really proud of myself, having a quick witty solution, even when smashed, to escape a possible conflict.

Next morning, the wife asked me what time I got in and I told her 12 o'clock. She didn't seem disturbed at all. Whew! Got away with that one! She then told me that we needed a new cuckoo clock. When I asked her why she said, "Well, it cuckooed three times, said 'oh fuck,' cuckooed four more times, cleared its throat, cuckooed another three times, giggled, cuckooed twice more, and then farted."

HEARING

A man is telling his neighbour, "I just bought a new hearing aid. It cost me £4,000 and it's proper state-of-the-art."
"Really?" answers the neighbour. "What kind is it?"
"Half past 12."

UN JOKE OR UNE JOKE?

A language instructor was explaining to her class that in French, nouns, unlike their English counterparts, are grammatically designated as masculine or feminine. For instance, "house" in French is feminine (une maison), while "pencil" is masculine (un crayon). One student then asked her what gender the word computer (ordinateur) was. She didn't know, so she decided to split the class into two, for fun, so that they could argue for it. Both groups were required to give four reasons for their recommendation.

The men's group decided that computers should definitely be of the feminine gender (une ordinateur), because:

1. No-one but their creator understands their internal logic, and even then it's only partially.
2. The native language they use to communicate with other computers is incomprehensible to everyone else.
3. Even the smallest mistakes are stored in long-term memory for later retrieval.
4. As soon as you make a commitment to one, you find yourself spending half your pay check on accessories for it.

The women's group, however, concluded that computers should be masculine (un ordinateur), because:

1. In order to do anything with them, you have to turn them on.
2. They have a lot of data but still can't think for themselves.
3. They are supposed to help you solve problems, but half the time they ARE the problem.
4. As soon as you commit to one, you realise that if you'd waited a little longer, you could have gotten a better model.

The women won.

ONE, TWO, THREE

A blonde, a brunette and a redhead all work at the same office for a female boss who always goes home early. "Hey, girls," says the brunette, "let's go home early tomorrow. She'll never know." So the next day, they all leave right after the boss does.

The brunette gets some extra gardening done, the redhead goes to a bar, and the blonde goes home to find her husband having sex with the female boss! She quietly sneaks out of the house, and the later returns home at her more normal time. The next morning at work, they discuss the previous afternoon. "That was fun," says the brunette. "We should do it again sometime."

"No way," says the blonde. "I almost got caught."

THE TEN THINGS MEN KNOW (FOR SURE) ABOUT WOMEN!!!

1.
2.
3.
4.
5.
6.
7.
8.
9.
10. They got boobs!

DEATH BY REPETITION

Brenda O'Malley is home making dinner, as usual, when Tom Finnegan arrives at her door. "Brenda, may I come in?" he asks. "I've something to tell ya."

"Of course you can come in, you're always welcome, Tom. But where's my husband?"

"That's what I'm here to be tellin'ya, Brenda. There was an accident down at the Guinness brewery..."

"Oh, God no!" cries Brenda. "Please don't tell me.."

"I must, Brenda. Your husband Shamus is dead and gone. I'm sorry."

Finally, she looked up at Tom. "How did it happen, Tom?"

"It was terrible, Brenda. He fell into a vat of Guinness, and drowned."

"Oh my dear Jesus! But you must tell me true, Tom. Did he at least go quickly?"

"Well, no Brenda, no. Fact is, he got out three times to pee."

SCREW YOU!

A man walks into a bar one night. He goes up to the bartender and asks for a beer. "Certainly, sir," replies the bartender. "That'll be one penny."

"One penny?!" exclaims the customer.

The barman replies, "Yes."

So the guy glances over the menu and asks, "Could I have a nice juicy T-bone steak with chips, peas and a fried egg?"

"Certainly, sir," replies the bartender, "but all that comes to real money."

"How much money?"

"Four pence," the bartender replies.

"Four pence!?" exclaims the guy. "Where's the guy who owns this place?"

The bartender replies, "Upstairs with my wife."

"What's he doing with your wife?"

"Same thing I'm doing with his business."

BECKHAM'S FLASK

David Beckham goes shopping, and sees something interesting in the kitchen department of a large department store. "What's that?" he asks.

"A Thermos flask," replies the assistant.

"What does it do?" asks Becks. The assistant tells him it keeps hot things hot and cold things cold. Really impressed, Beckham buys one and takes it along to his next training session. "Here, boys, look at this," Beckham says proudly. "It's a Thermos flask."

The lads are impressed. "What does it do?" they ask.
"It keeps hot things hot and cold things cold," says David.
"And what have you got in it?" asks Roy Keane.
"Two cups of coffee and a choc ice," replies David.

LITERALLY A SICK JOKE

Two rats are living in a sewer. One rat turns to the other and says "I'm sick of this."
"Sick of what?" asks the other rat.
"Sick of having shit for breakfast, shit for lunch, shit for dinner, shit for tea... shit all day long. I'm just sick of it."
"Don't worry," replies his mate. "I know how to cheer you up. Tonight we'll go on the piss."

MOTHER-IN-LAW JOKE

A man was leaving a cafe with his morning coffee when he noticed a most unusual funeral procession approaching the cemetery. A long black hearse was followed by a second hearse. Behind the second hearse was a solitary man walking a pit bull on a leash. Behind him was a queue of 200 men walking in single file. The man couldn't stand the curiosity, he respectfully approached the man walking the dog, "I am so sorry for your loss, and I know now is a bad time to disturb you, but I've never seen a funeral like this with so many people walking in single file. Whose funeral is it?"

The man replied "Well that first hearse is for my wife."

"What happened to her?"

"My dog attacked and killed her."

He enquired further. "Well, who is in the second hearse then?"

"The mother-in-law. She tried to save my wife and, lo and behold, the dog turned on her and killed her as well."

A poignant moment of silence passed between the men. "Can I borrow the dog?"

"Yeah, of course you can mate, but you'll have to join the queue!"

BEAVER SHOOTING

A 90-year-old man goes to a doctor for his annual check-up. The doctor asks him how he's feeling. The 90-year-old says, "I've never felt better. I have an 18-year-old bride who is pregnant with my child. What do you think about that?"

The doctor considers his question for a minute and begins: "I have a friend who is an avid hunter and never misses a season. One day when he was going out in a bit of a hurry, he accidentally picked up his umbrella instead of his gun. When he got to the creek, he saw a beaver sitting beside the stream of water. He raised his umbrella and went 'bang, bang,' and the beaver fell over dead. What do you think of that?"

The 90-year-old said, "I'd say somebody else shot that beaver."

"My point exactly!"

CORPORATE LESSON 1

Case: Usually the staff of the company play football. The middle level managers are more interested in tennis. The top management usually has a preference for golf.

Analysis: As you go up the corporate ladder, the balls reduce in size.

DRIVEN MAD

Thank you for telephoning the Mental Health Hotline.

For obsessive-compulsive disorders, please press 1 repeatedly.

For depression, please don't both pressing 2. It won't make any difference. They won't be able to help you, and you'll still feel like shit anyway.

For co-dependency issues, please ask someone to press 3 for you.

For multiple-personality disorder, please press 4, 5 and 6.

For delusions, please press 7 and your call will be transferred to the mothership.

For amnesia, please press 8 and state your name, address, telephone number, date and time of birth, mother's maiden name, and the names of the current and former leaders of your country.

For dyslexia, please press 9361895873921.

For post-traumatic stress disorder, please press 0 very slowly and carefully, remaining calm and relaxed, and thinking pleasant, soothing thoughts.

For short-term memory loss problems, please press the * key.

For short-term memory loss problems, please press the * key.

For short-term memory loss problems, please press the * key.

For nervous tension, please fiddle uneasily with the # key until a representative is available to talk to you.

For mania, please thump as many buttons as quickly as you possibly can.

For paranoid schizophrenia, please press the button that the voices in your head tell you to press.

For paranoia and persecution syndromes, please stay on the line. We know exactly where you are and what you want, and we'll be coming for you any moment now. Your new hair-do really doesn't suit you, by the way.

For low self-esteem and confidence disorders, please hang up. Everyone is far too busy and important to talk to you.

For rage and buried anger issues, please smash the telephone against the wall repeatedly, shrieking at the top of your lungs.

For sociopathy and violent psychopathic syndrome, please dismantle the telephone carefully into its component pieces with a sharp scalpel, wrap each chunk in a separate weighted plastic bag, and scatter the pieces in a large body of water. Remember to wear gloves throughout.

For temporal uncertainty syndrome, please leave a message after the beep or before the beep or please leave a message after the beep. Please, wait for the beep.

Finally, for hysteria, DON'T TOUCH A THING! Something TERRIBLE might happen.

FUN AT THE OFFICE (OR 34 WAYS TO ANNOY PEOPLE -- TRY SENDING THEM STUPID JOKE EMAILS FOR A START...!)

1. Leave the photocopier set to reduce 200%, extra dark, 17-inch paper, 99 copies.
2. Develop an unnatural fear of staplers.
3. Every time someone asks you to do something, ask if they want fries with that.
4. If you have a glass eye, tap on it with your pen while talking to others.
5. Insist that your email address is emperor-of-the-zorg@companyname.com.
6. Encourage your colleagues to join you in a little synchronised chair-dancing.
7. Reply to everything someone says with "That's what YOU think."
8. Practice making fax and modem noises.
9. Highlight irrelevant material in scientific websites and cc: it to your boss.
10. Make beeping noises when a large person backs up.
11. Finish all your sentences with the words "in accordance with prophecy".
12. Signal that a conversation is over by clamping your hands over your ears.
13. Disassemble your pen and "accidentally" flip the cartridge across the room.
14. Holler random numbers while someone is counting.
15. Adjust the tint on your monitor so that all people are green and insist to others that you like it that way.
16. Staple papers in the middle of the page.
17. Publicly investigate just how slowly you can make a croaking noise.
18. Wave to strangers from your office window.
19. Put decaf in the coffee maker for three weeks. Once everyone has gotten over their caffeine addictions, switch to espresso.
20. TYPE ONLY IN UPPERCASE.
21. type only in lowercase.
22. Don't use any punctuation anytime anywhere ever and I mean never do you understand
23. Buy a large quantity of orange traffic cones and re-route the office.
24. Repeat the following conversation a dozen times: "Do you hear that?", "What?", "Never mind, it's gone now."
25. As much as possible, skip rather than walk.
26. Try playing the William Tell overture (the Lone Ranger theme) by tapping on the bottom of your chin. When nearly done, announce "No, wait I messed it up," and repeat.
27. Ask people what sex they are. Laugh hysterically after they answer.
28. While making presentations, occasionally bob your head like a parakeet.
29. In the memo field of all your checks, write "for sensual massage".
30. Stomp on little plastic ketchup packets.
31. Send email to the rest of the company to tell them what you're doing. For example, "If anyone needs me, I'll be in the bathroom, in Stall #3."

32. Ask your co-workers mysterious questions and then scribble the answers in a notebook. Mutter something about "psychological profiles".

34. Tell your boss, "It's not the voices in my head that bother me, it's the voices in your head."

A NICE PLACE FOR A DRINK

A Scotsman, an Italian, and an Irishman are in a bar. They are having a good time and all agree that the bar is a nice place. Then the Scotsman says, "Aye, this is a nice bar, but where I come from, back in Glasgee, there's a better one. At MacDougal's, ye buy a drink, ye buy another drink, and MacDougal himself will buy yir third drink!"

The others agree that sounds like a good place. Then the Italian says, "Yeah, dat's a nice-a bar, but where I come from, dere's a better one. In Roma, dere's dis place, Vincenzo's. At Vincenzo's, you buy a drinka, Vincenzo buys you a drinka. You buy anudda drinka, Vincenzo buys you anudda drinka."

Everyone agrees that sounds like a great bar. Then the Irishman says, "You tink dat's great? Where Oi come from in Dublin, dere's dis place called Morphy's. At Morphy's, they boi you your first drink, dey boi you yer second drink, den dey boi you yer tird drink, and den, after all dat, dey take you out de back and get you laid!"

"Wow!" say the other two. "That's fantastic! Did that actually happen to you?"

"No," says the Irish guy, "but it happened to me sister!"

HOW TO TELL YOU'RE IN
SOUTHERN CALIFORNIA:

- Your co-worker tells you he/she has eight body piercings. None are visible.
- You make over $250,000 and still can't afford a house.
- Your child's third-grade teacher has purple hair, a nose ring and is named Breeze.
- You can't remember... is pot illegal?
- You've been to more than one baby shower where the father is a sperm donor.
- A really great parking space can move you to tears.
- A low-speed police pursuit can interrupt any TV broadcast.
- You assume every company offers domestic partner benefits, a fabulous exercise facility and tofu takeout.
- You're thinking of taking an adult class but you can't decide between aromatherapy and conversational Mandarin.
- Your best friends just named their twins after her acting coach and his personal trainer.
- It's sprinkling and every news station is running continual 'STORM WATCH' alerts.
- The three-hour traffic jam you just sat through wasn't caused by a horrific nine-car pile-up, but by everyone slowing to rubberneck a lost shoe laying on the shoulder.

OOH, NASTY!

At the exact same time, there are two young men on opposite sides of the earth. One is walking a tight rope between two skyscrapers, the other is getting a blow job from an 85-year-old woman. They are each thinking the exact same thing.
Q: What are they both thinking?
A: Don't look down.

HEALTHCARE

The Queen was visiting one of London's top hospitals and she specified she wanted to see absolutely everything. During her tour of the floors she passed a room where a male patient was having a wank. "Oh my," said the Queen. "That's disgraceful, what is the meaning of this?"

The Doctor leading the tour explains. "I am sorry your Majesty, but this man has a very serious medical condition and is only following doctors' orders. His body produces too much semen, and his testicles keep overfilling. Until we can find out exactly what is causing this problem he's been instructed to do that at least five times a day or there is a danger that his testicles will explode and he will die instantly."

"Oh, I am sorry," said the Queen. On the next floor they passed a room where a sexy young nurse was giving a patient a blow job. "Oh my," said the Queen. "What's happening in there?"
The Doctor replied, "Same problem, but he's with BUPA".

THINGS YOU PROBABLY DIDN'T KNOW WERE TRUE

Mosquito repellents don't repel! They hide you. The spray blocks the mosquitos' sensors so they don't know you're there.

Dentists have recommended that a toothbrush be kept at least six feet away from the nearest toilet to avoid airborne particles resulting from the flush.

The liquid inside young coconuts can be used as substitute for blood plasma.

No piece of paper, whatever its thickness, can be hand-folded in half more than nine times

Donkeys kill more people annually than plane crashes.

You burn more calories sleeping than you do watching television.

Oak trees do not produce acorns until they are 50 years of age or older.

The first product to have a barcode was Wrigley's gum.

The King of Hearts is the only playing-card king without a moustache.

A Boeing 747s wingspan is longer than the Wright brother's first flight.

Venus is the only planet that rotates clockwise.

Apples are more efficient at waking you up in the morning than caffeine is.

The plastic things on the end of shoelaces are called aglets.

Most dust particles in your house are made from dead skin.

Marilyn Monroe had six toes.

All US presidents have worn glasses. Some just didn't like being seen wearing them in public.

Walt Disney was afraid of mice.

Intelligent women are more likely to pick a heavier partner than dumb women, and are more likely to have a successful relationship as a result.

Pearls melt in vinegar.

Thirty-five percent of the people who use personal ads for dating are already married.

The three most valuable brand names on earth are Marlboro, Coca-Cola, and Budweiser, in that order.

It is possible to lead a cow upstairs....but not downstairs.

The reason firehouses have circular stairways is from the days when the engines were pulled by horses. The horses were stabled on the ground floor and figured out how to walk up straight staircases.

Richard Millhouse Nixon was the first US president whose name contained all the letters from the word "criminal." The second was William Jefferson Clinton.

Turtles can breathe through their butts.

Butterflies taste with their feet.

In ten minutes, a hurricane releases more energy than the entire world's nuclear weapons combined.

On average, 100 people choke to death on ballpoint pens every year.

On average people fear spiders more than they do death.

Ninety percent of New York City cabbies are recently arrived immigrants.

Elephants are the only animals that can't jump.

Only one person in two billion will live to be 116 or older.

Women blink nearly twice as much as men.

It's physically impossible for you to lick your elbow.

French women are 62% more sexy than Italian women.

The Main Library at Indiana University sinks over an inch every year because when it was built, engineers failed to take into account the weight of all the books that would occupy the building.

A snail can sleep for three years.

The skin on your elbow has no feeling. Pinch it and see.

No word in the English language rhymes with "month".

The average life span of a major league baseball is just seven pitches

Our eyes are always the same size from birth, but our nose and ears never stop growing. SCARY!!!

The electric chair was invented by a dentist.

The most popular cheese in the world is reblochon.

All polar bears are left-handed.

In ancient Egypt, priests plucked EVERY hair from their bodies, including their eyebrows and eyelashes.

An ostrich's eye is bigger than its brain.

Sheep won't eat glass (so they're not THAT dumb, then!).

"Typewriter" is the longest word that can be made using the letters only on one row of the keyboard.

"Go" is the shortest complete sentence in the English language.

A crocodile cannot stick its tongue out.

The cigarette lighter was invented before the match.

Americans on average eat 18 acres of pizza every day.

Most people who read this email will try to lick their elbow.

PS did you try to lick your elbow???

THE MIRROR OF TRUTH

A brunette, redhead and blonde went to a fitness spa for some fun and relaxation. After a stimulating healthy lunch, all three decided to visit the ladies' room and found a strange-looking woman sitting at the entrance who said, "Welcome to the ladies' room. Be sure to check out our newest feature – a mirror which, if you look into it and say something truthful, will reward you with a wish. But, be warned, if you say something false, you will be sucked into the mirror to live in a void of nothingness for all eternity!"

The three women quickly entered and upon finding the mirror, the brunette said, "I think I'm the most talented of us three." In an instant she was surrounded by a pile of money.

The redhead stepped up and said, "I think I'm the most beautiful of us three," and she suddenly found the keys to a brand new Jaguar in her hands.

Excited over the possibility of having a wish come true, the blonde looked into the mirror and said, "I think..." and was promptly sucked into the mirror.

FLYBOY FUN

"Squawks" are problems noted by U.S. Air Force pilots and left for maintenance crews to fix before the next flight. Here are some actual complaints logged by Air Force pilots and the replies from the maintenance crew. (C) = complaint, (S) = solution

(C) Left inside main tyre almost needs replacement
(S) Almost replaced left inside main tyre
(C) Test flight OK, except auto land very rough
(S) Auto land not installed on this aircraft
(C) No. 2 propeller seeping prop fluid
(S) No. 2 propeller seepage normal – Nos. 1, 3 and 4 propellers lack normal seepage
(C) Something loose in cockpit
(S) Something tightened in cockpit
(C) Evidence of leak in right main landing gear
(S) Evidence removed

(C) DME volume unbelievably loud
(S) Volume set to believable level
(C) Dead bugs on windshield
(S) Live bugs have been ordered
(C) Autopilot in altitude hold mode produces a 200 fpm descent
(S) Cannot reproduce the problem on ground
(C) IFF inoperative
(S) IFF always inoperative in OFF mode

(C) Friction locks cause throttle levers to stick
(S) That is what they are there for
(C) No. 3 engine missing
(S) Engine found on right wing after brief search
(C) Aircraft handles funny
(S) Aircraft warned to "fly properly and be serious"
(C) Target radar hums
(S) Target radar programmed with proper words

FREEZE!

A woman was in bed with her lover when she heard her husband opening the front door. "Hurry!" she said. "Stand in the corner!" She quickly rubbed baby oil all over him and then she dusted him with talcum powder. "Don't move until I tell you to," she whispered. "Just pretend you're a statue."

"What's this, honey?" the husband inquired as he entered the room.
"Oh, it's just a statue," she replied nonchalantly. "The Smiths bought one for their bedroom. I liked it so much, I got one for us, too."

No more was said about the statue, not even later that night when they went to sleep. Around 2am, the husband got out of bed, went to the kitchen and returned a while later with a sandwich and a glass of milk. "Here," he said to the statue, "eat something. I stood like an idiot at the Smiths' for three days, and nobody offered me as much as a glass of water."

SUBTLE STORY

Little Johnny is excited because the circus has come to town and his Mum has got front row tickets for him. Finally the evening come and little Johnny and his Mum go off to the big top. Little Johnny sits there and enjoys the lions and the tigers and the jugglers and the trapeze artists, and finally, out come little Johnny's favourites, the clowns.
Johnny loves the clowns and their humorous japes until one of the clowns comes up to him and says, "Little boy, are you the front end of an ass?"
"No," replies little Johnny.
"Are you the rear end of an ass?"
"No," replies little Johnny again.
"In that case," says the clown, "you must be no end of an ass!"
Laughter fills the big top, little Johnny is distraught, and he runs out of the circus and all the way home in tears. When his Mum catches up with him, she says, "Little Johnny, don't worry, your Uncle Marvo, the master of lightning wit, backchat and repartee, is coming to stay tomorrow. We will take him to the circus and he will sort that nasty clown out." At this news, little Johnny cheers, and starts looking forward to the next night.

The next night comes and, sure enough, Uncle Marvo, the master of lightning wit, backchat and repartee arrives and the three of them set off for the circus. When they get there, little Johnny, his Mum and Uncle Marvo, the master of lightning wit, backchat and repartee sit down and enjoy the lions, the tigers, the jugglers and the trapeze artists and then out come the clowns. Again, little Johnny is enjoying their antics and again, one of the clowns comes up to him and says, "Little boy, are you the front end of an ass?"

"No," replies little Johnny.

"Are you the rear end of an ass?"

"No," replies little Johnny again.

"In that case," says the clown, "you must be no end of an ass!"

Laughter fills the big top once more and as little Johnny jumps up, quick as a flash, Uncle Marvo, the master of lightning wit, backchat and repartee jumps up and shouts at the very top of his voice "Fuck off, you red nosed bastard!"

MONKEYS

A lorry driver breaks down on the M6 with a cargo of live monkeys on board, bound for Chester Zoo. They need to be delivered by 9am and the driver fears he will get the sack if they don't get there on time. He decides to try and thumb a lift for his monkeys, and eventually an Irish lorry driver pulls over. "Where they going?" asks the Irish chap.

"Do us a favour mate and take these to Chester Zoo for me," says the driver, "and here's a hundred quid for your troubles." "Happy days," says the Irish guy. He loads the monkeys onto his truck and gets on his way. The lorry driver goes about trying to fix his truck and is there for a good few hours when he notices the Irish guy coming back down the motorway, still with all the monkeys on board.

Panicking, he flags him down again. "What are you playing at?" he fumes. "I told you to take them to Chester Zoo!"

" I did," the other says. "There's still fifty quid left, so now we're going to Alton Towers."

CORPORATE LESSON 2

Case: A priest was driving along and saw a young nun on the side of the road. He stopped and offered her a lift which she accepted. She got in and crossed her legs, forcing her gown to open and reveal a lovely leg. The priest had a look and nearly had an accident.

After controlling the car, he stealthily slid his hand up her leg. The nun looked at him and immediately said, "Father, remember psalm 129?" The priest was flustered and apologised profusely. He forced himself to remove his hand. However, he was unable to remove his eyes from her leg.

Further on while changing gear, he let his hand slide up her leg again. The nun once again said, "Father, remember psalm 129?" Once again the priest apologized. "Sorry Sister, but the flesh is weak." Arriving at the convent, the nun got out, gave him a meaningful glance and went on her way. On his arrival at the church, the priest rushed to retrieve a bible and looked up psalm 129. It said, "Go forth and seek, further up you will find glory."

Analysis: Always be well informed in your job, or you might miss a great opportunity.

ETHICS

Here are two ethical questions:

Q1: If you knew a woman who was pregnant, who already had eight kids, three of whom were deaf, two of whom were blind and one of whom was mentally retarded, and she had syphilis, would you recommend that she have an abortion?
Read the next question before scrolling down to the answer of this one.

Q2: It is time to elect the world leader, and your vote is the decider. Here are the facts about the three leading candidates: Candidate A associates with crooked politicians and consults with astrologists. He's had two mistresses. He also chain smokes and drinks eight to ten martinis a day.

Candidate B was kicked out of office twice, sleeps until noon, used opium in college and drinks a quart of whisky every evening.

Candidate C is a decorated war hero. He's a vegetarian, doesn't smoke, drinks an occasional beer and hasn't had any extramarital affairs.

Which of these candidates would be your choice?
Decide first, no peeking, then scroll down for the answer.
Candidate A is Franklin D. Roosevelt
Candidate B is Winston Churchill
Candidate C is Adolph Hitler
... and by the way, if you said yes to the abortion question, you just killed Beethoven.

NIGHTMARES

Nightmare 1
After a long night of lovemaking, the young guy rolls over, pulls out a cigarette from his jeans and searches for his lighter. Unable to find it, he asks the girl if she has one at hand. "There might be some matches in the top drawer," she replies. He opens the drawer of the bedside table and find a box of matches sitting neatly on top of a framed picture of another man. Naturally, the guy begins to worry. "Is this your husband?" he inquires nervously.
"No, silly," she replies, snuggling up to him.
"Your boyfriend then?" he asks.
"No, not at all," she says, nibbling away at his ear.
"Well, who is he then?"
"That's me before the operation."

Nightmare 2
The spark had been lost in this guy's marriage, so he was trying to think of a way to rekindle

it. One night he came home from work and found his wife asleep in bed. After pondering for a moment, he proceeded to get under the covers and go down on his wife. Soon she began to gently squirm and moan in pleasure. After a few minutes, her body arched with ecstasy as she climaxed. Afterwards, the man went straight to the bathroom to brush his teeth. When he got there, the light was on and he saw his wife there shaving her legs.

"What are you doing in here?!?", he exclaimed.

"Shhhh!," she said, pointing at the bed, "You'll wake your mother up."

Nightmare 3

One night a guy takes his girlfriend home. As they are about to kiss each other goodnight at the front door, the guy starts feeling a little horny. With an air of confidence, he leans with his hand against the wall and, smiling, he says to her, "Babe, would you give me a blow job?"

Horrified, she replies, "Are you mad? My parents will see us!"

"Oh come on! Who's going to see us at this hour?" He asks, grinning at her.

"No, please. Can you imagine if we get caught?"

"Oh come on! There's nobody around, they're all sleeping!"

"No way. It's just too risky!"

"Oh please, please, I love you so much!"

"No, no, and no. I love you too, but I just can't!"

"Oh yes you can. Please?"

Out of the blue, the light on the stairs goes on and the girl's sister shows up in her pyjamas, hair dishevelled, and in a sleepy voice she says, "Dad says to go ahead and give him his blow job. If you're really not in the mood, then I suppose I can do it for you. If it's absolutely necessary, Mum says she can come down and do it herself. But for God's sake please get him to take his hand off the intercom first!"

I LOVE YOUR KNEES...

A young man moved into a new apartment on his own and went to the lobby to put his name on his mailbox. While there, an attractive young lady wearing a robe came out of the apartment next to the mailboxes. The young lad smiled at the woman and she started a conversation with him. As they talked, her robe slipped open and it was obvious that she had nothing else on.

The poor lad broke into a sweat trying to maintain eye contact. After a few minutes, she placed her hand on his arm, then said, "I hear someone coming, let's go to my apartment."

He followed her into her apartment; she closed the door and leaned against it, allowing her robe to fall off completely. Now naked, she purred at him, "What would you say is my best feature?"
Flustered and embarrassed, he finally squeaked, "It's got to be your ears!"

Astounded, and a little hurt she asked, "My ears? Look at my tits, they are full and 100% natural! I work out every day! My ass is firm and solid! Look at my skin, no blemishes anywhere! You can see I've got a Brazilian. How can you think that my ears are the best part of my body?"
Clearing his throat, he stammered, "Well, it's just that outside, when you said you heard someone coming? That was me."

HOW TO ADMINISTER A PILL TO A CAT

For cat owners everywhere:
1. Pick up the cat and cradle it in the crook of your left arm as if holding a baby. Position right forefinger and thumb on either side of cat's mouth and gently apply pressure to cheeks while holding pill in right hand. As cat opens mouth, pop pill into mouth.
2. Allow cat to close mouth and swallow.
3. Retrieve pill from floor and cat from behind sofa. Cradle cat in left arm and repeat process.
4. Retrieve cat from bedroom and throw away soggy pill.
5. Take new pill from foil wrap, cradle cat in left arm, holding rear paws tightly with left hand. Force jaws open and push pill to back of mouth with right forefinger. Hold mouth shut for a count of ten.
6. Retrieve pill from goldfish bowl and cat from top of wardrobe. Call partner in from garden.
7. Kneel on floor with cat wedged firmly between knees, hold front and rear paws. Ignore growls emitted by cat. Get spouse to hold cat's head firmly with one hand while forcing wooden ruler into mouth. Drop pill down ruler and rub cat's throat vigorously.

8. Retrieve cat from curtain rail, get another pill from foil wrap. Make note to buy new ruler and repair curtains. Carefully sweep shattered figurines and vases from hearth and set to one side for gluing later.

9. Wrap cat in a large towel and get spouse to lie on cat with cat's head just visible from below armpit. Put pill in end of a drinking straw, force cat's mouth open with pencil and blow down straw.

10. Check label to make sure pill is not harmful to humans, drink a beer to take away the taste. Apply Band-aid to partner's forearm and remove blood from the carpet with soap and water.

11. Retrieve cat from neighbour's shed. Get another pill. Open another beer. Place cat in cupboard and close door onto neck, so as to leave the head showing. Force mouth open with dessert spoon. Flick pill down throat with elastic band.

12. Fetch screwdriver from garage and put cupboard door back on hinges. Drink beer. Fetch scotch. Pour shot, drink. Apply cold compress to cheek and check date of last tetanus jab. Apply whisky compress to cheek to disinfect. Toss back another shot. Throw tee-shirt away and fetch new one from bedroom.

13. Ring fire brigade to retrieve the f*****g cat from tree across the road. Apologise to neighbour who crashed into fence while swerving to avoid cat. Take last pill from foil wrap.

14. Tie the little bastard's front paws to rear paws with garden twine and bind tightly to leg of the dining table. Find heavy pruning gloves from shed. Push pill into mouth followed by large piece of fillet steak. Be rough about it. Hold head vertical and pour two pints of water down cat's throat to wash down pill.

15. Consume remainder of scotch. Get spouse to drive you to the A&E, sit quietly while doctor stitches fingers and forearm and removes pill from your eye. Call furniture shop on way home to order a new table.

16. Arrange for RSPCA to collect the mutant cat from hell and ring local pet shop to see whether they have any guinea pigs.

HOW TO ADMINISTER A PILL TO A DOG

1. Wrap it in bacon.

NOW THIS IS A VERY SILLY ONE LOL...

A man is dining in a fancy restaurant and there is a gorgeous redhead sitting at the next table. He has been checking her out since he sat down, but lacks the nerve to talk with her. Suddenly she sneezes and her glass eye comes flying out of its socket towards the man. He reflexively reaches out, grabs it out of the air and hands it back.

"Oh my, I am sooo sorry," the woman says as she pops her eye back in place. "Let me buy your dinner to make it up to you," she says.

They enjoy a wonderful dinner together and afterwards the theatre followed by drinks. They talk, they laugh, she shares her deepest dreams and he shares his. After paying for everything, she asks him if he would like to come to her place for an intimate night-cap... and stay for breakfast the next morning. The next morning, she cooks a gourmet meal with all the trimmings.

The guy is amazed! Everything had been incredible. "You know," he said, "you are the perfect woman. Are you this nice to every guy you meet?"

"No", she replies. "You just happened to catch my eye."

MILKY MILKY

A woman and a baby were in the examining room waiting for the doctor. The doctor finally did arrive, examined the baby, checked her weight, found it somewhat below normal and asked if the baby was breast fed or bottle fed. "Breast fed," the woman replied.

"Well, strip down to your waist," the doctor ordered. She did. He pressed, kneaded, rolled, cupped and pinched both breasts for a while in a detailed, rigorously thorough examination. Motioning to her to get dressed, he said, "No wonder this baby is under-weight. You don't have any milk."

"I know," she said, "I'm his Grandma, but I'm glad I came."

YOUR MUM!

Three guys are drinking in a bar when a drunk comes in, staggers up to them, and points at the guy in the middle, shouting, "Your mom's the best shag in town!"

Everyone expects a fight, but the guy ignores him, so the drunk wanders off and bellies up to the bar at the far end. Ten minutes later, the drunk comes back, points at the same guy and says, "I just did your mom and it was s-w-e-e-t!"

Again the guy refuses to take the bait and the drunk goes back to the far end of the bar. Ten minutes later, he comes back and announces, "Your mom loved it when I gave it to her!"

Finally the guy interrupts. "Go home, Dad. You're drunk!"

YOUR BOY!

Stan was seconds away from receiving a vasectomy when his brother and sister-in-law barged in holding their newborn baby. "Stop! You can't do this!" exclaimed the brother.
"And why not?" asked Stan.
"Don't you want to have a beautiful baby someday like my wife and I have here?"
Stan said nothing.
The brother grew impatient, "C'mon Stan, I want a nephew. Stan, make me an uncle."
Stan couldn't take it anymore. He gave his sister-in-law an apologetic look and asked his brother, "You're sure you want a nephew?"
"Yes," the brother replied. "It would be an honour."
"Well congratulations. You're holding him."

TIP OF THE SLONGUE

A guy with a black eye boards his plane and sits down in his seat. He notices immediately that the guy next to him has a black eye too. He says to him, "Hey this is a coincidence, we both have black eyes. Mind if I ask how you got yours?"

The other guy says, "Well, it just happened. It was an accidental Freudian slip. See, I was at the ticket counter and this gorgeous blonde with the most massive breasts in the world was there. So, instead of saying, I'd like two tickets to Pittsburgh,' I accidentally said, 'I'd like two pickets to Tittsburgh.' She socked me a good one."

The first guy replied, "Wow! This is unbelievable. Mine was a Freudian Slip too. I was at the breakfast table this morning and I wanted to say to my wife, 'Please pour me a bowl of Frosties, honey,' but instead I accidentally said, 'You've ruined my fucking life, you fat, evil slag.'"

BROADBAND TO HEAVEN

An American decided to write a book about famous churches around the world. For his first chapter he decided to write about famous English and Scottish cathedrals. So he bought a plane ticket and made the trip to London, thinking that he would work his way northwards.

On his first day, he was inside a church taking photographs when he noticed a golden telephone mounted on the wall with a sign that read '£10,000 per call'. The American, being intrigued, asked a priest who was strolling by what the telephone was used for. The priest replied that it was a direct line to heaven and that for £10,000 you could talk to God. The American thanked the priest and went along his way. Next stop was in Salisbury. There, at a very large cathedral, he saw the same golden telephone with the same sign under it. He wondered if this was the same kind of telephone he saw in London and he asked a nearby nun what its purpose was. She told him that it was a direct line to heaven and that for £10,000 he could talk to God. "OK, thank you," said the American.

He then travelled to Bath, Coventry, York and Newcastle and in every church he saw the same golden telephone with the same '£10,000 per call' sign under it. With his book going well, he left England and travelled north to Scotland. Again, at his first stop at St. Giles Cathedral in Edinburgh, there was the same golden telephone, but this time the sign under it read '10p per call.'

The American was surprised so he asked the minister about the sign. "Vicar, I've travelled all over England and I've seen this same golden telephone in many cathedrals and churches. I'm told that it is a direct line to heaven, but in all the cities in England the price was £10,000 per call. Why is it so cheap here?"

The minister smiled and answered, "You're in Scotland now, my child. It's a local call".

HAR HAR... I LOVE THIS ONE...

A married couple was in a terrible accident where the woman's face was severely burned. The doctor told the husband that they couldn't graft any skin from her body because she was too skinny. The husband nicely offered to donate some of his own skin. However, the only skin on his body that the doctor felt was suitable would have to come from his buttocks. The husband and wife agreed that they would tell no one about where the skin came from and requested that the doctor also honour their secret. After all, this was a very delicate matter.

After the surgery was completed, everyone was astounded at the woman's new beauty. She looked even more beautiful than she ever had before! All her friends and relatives just went on and on about her youthful beauty. One day, she was alone with her husband and she was overcome with emotion at his sacrifice. She said, "Dear, I just want to thank you for everything you did for me. There is no way I could ever repay you."

"My darling," he replied, "I get all the thanks I need every time I see your mother kiss you on the cheek."

DUCK

A duck walks into a pub and says to the barman,
"Got any bread?"
"No."
"Got any bread?"
"No."

"Got any bread?"
"No, we have no bread."
"Got any bread?"
"No, we haven't got any bread."
"Got any bread?"
"No! Are you deaf? We haven't got any sodding bread. Ask me again and I'll nail your damn beak to the bar, you irritating bloody bird!"
"Got any nails?"
"What? No."
"Got any bread?"

AND HERE GOES ANOTHER ONE

Two brooms were hanging in the closet and after a while, they got to know each other so well, they decided to get married. One broom was, of course, the bride broom... and the other the groom broom. The bride broom looked very beautiful in her white dress. The groom broom was handsome and suave in his tuxedo. The wedding was lovely.

Afterward, at the wedding dinner, the bride broom leaned over and said to the groom broom, "I think I am going to have a little baby broom!"

"Impossible!" said the groom broom, "we haven't even swept together!"

THE RUBBER CASE

A husband and wife are waiting at the bus stop, with them are their eight children. A blind man joins them after a few minutes. When the bus arrives, it is already busy, and only the wife and her eight children are able to fit on the bus. So the husband and the blind man decide to walk.

After a while the husband gets irritated by the ticking of the stick of the blind man and says to him, "Why don't you put a piece of rubber on the end of your stick? That clicking sound is driving me crazy!"

The blind man replies, "If you'd have put a rubber on the end of YOUR stick, we'd be sitting on the bus, so shut up!"

NOTES AND QUERIES

If you take an Oriental person and spin him around several times, does he become disoriented?
If people from Poland are called Poles, why aren't people from Holland called Holes?
Why do we say something is out of whack? What's a whack?
Do infants enjoy infancy as much as adults enjoy adultery?
If a pig loses its voice, is it disgruntled?
If love is blind, why is lingerie so popular?
When someone asks you, "A penny for your thoughts" and you put your two cents in ... what happens to the other penny?
Why is the man who invests all your money called a broker?
Why do croutons come in airtight packages? Aren't they just stale bread to begin with?
When cheese gets its picture taken, what does it say?
Why is a person who plays the piano called a pianist but a person who drives a race car not called a racist?
Why are a wise man and a wise guy opposites?
Why do overlook and oversee mean opposite things?
Why isn't the number 11 pronounced onety one?
"I am" is reportedly the shortest sentence in the English language. Could it be that "I do" is the longest sentence?
If lawyers are disbarred and clergymen defrocked, doesn't it follow that electricians can be delighted, musicians denoted and cowboys deranged?
If FedEx and UPS were to merge, would they call it Fed UP?
Do Lipton Tea employees take coffee breaks?

What hair colour do they put on the driver's licenses of bald men?

Why do people seem to read the Bible a whole lot more as they get older? Is it because they're cramming for their final exam?

Western mothers feed their babies with tiny little spoons and forks. What do Chinese mothers use? Toothpicks?

Why do they put pictures of criminals up in the post office? What are we supposed to do, write to them? Why don't they just put their pictures on the postage stamps so the mailmen can look for them while they deliver the mail?

If it's true that we are here to help others, then what exactly are the others here for?

You never really learn to swear until you learn to drive.

No one ever says "It's only a game" when their team is winning.

Ever wonder what the speed of lightning would be if it didn't zigzag?

Last night I played a blank tape at full blast. The mime next door went nuts.

If a cow laughed, would milk come out of her nose?

Whatever happened to Preparations A through G?

Isn't making a smoking section in a restaurant like making a peeing section in a swimming pool?

If the Jacksonville Jaguars are known as the "Jags" and the Tampa Bay Buccaneers are known as the "Bucs", what does that make the Tennessee Titans?

If four out of five people suffer from diarrhoea, does that mean that one enjoys it?

SNAPPIES

Romeo Beckham gets his first chance to play for Man U at Old Trafford, so he asks his dad what number he should wear. His dad thinks for a minute and says: "Wear 4 out there, Romeo."

A man goes to a fancy dress party dressed only in his Y-fronts. A woman comes up to him and says 'What are you supposed to be?' 'A premature ejaculation,' the guy replies. 'What?' 'Yeah, look, I've just come in my pants.'

Two aerials met on a roof, fell in love and got married. The ceremony was rubbish but the reception was brilliant.

Two cannibals are eating a clown. One says to the other, 'Does this taste funny to you?'

A man with a strawberry stuck up his bum goes to the doc. The doc says, 'I'll give you some cream to put on that.'

NUFFIN' I CAN'T HANDEL

Stephen Spielberg is casting for a new film based around the great composers. Anyway to give the film a twist and some oomph, he decides to cast the parts to the great action heroes of today. He calls Stallone, Arnie, Bruce Willis and Steven Seagal into his office to hear who they would like to play.

"Well," started Stallone, "I've always admired Mozart. I would love to play him."
"Chopin has always been my favourite, and my image would improve if people saw me playing the piano," said Willis. "I'll play him."

"I've always been partial to Strauss and his waltzes," said Seagal. "I'd like to play him."
Spielberg was very pleased with these choices. "Sounds splendid."
Then, looking at Schwarzenegger, he asked, "Who do you want to be, Arnold?"
Arnold says, "I'll be Bach."

DIVORCEE BARBIE

A man was driving home one evening and realised that it was his daughter's birthday and he hadn't bought her a present. He drove to the shopping centre and ran to the toy shop and he asked the manager, "How much is that new Barbie in the window?"

The Manager replied, "Which one? We have 'Barbie goes to the gym' for £19.95, 'Barbie goes to the Ball' for £19.95, 'Barbie goes shopping' for £19.95, 'Barbie goes to the beach' for £19.95, 'Barbie goes to the Nightclub' for £19.95 and "Divorced Barbie' for £399.95."

"Why is the Divorced Barbie £399.95, when all the others are £19.95?" the dad asked."

"'Divorced Barbie' comes with Ken's car, Ken's House, Ken's boat, Ken's dog, Ken's cat and Ken's furniture," replied the shop manager.

THIS IS MY TOWN

IMPEACHABLE LOGIC

Two builders (Dave and Stuart) are seated either side of a table in a rough pub when a well-dressed man enters, orders a beer and sits on a stool at the bar. The two builders start to speculate about the occupation of the man in the suit.

"I reckon he's an accountant", Dave says.

Stuart says "No way – he's a stockbroker."

"He ain't no stockbroker ! A stockbroker wouldn't come in here!"

The argument repeats itself for some time until the volume of beer gets the better of Dave and he makes for the toilet. On entering the toilet he sees that the suit is standing at a urinal. Curiosity and the several beers get the better of the builder. "Scuse me.... no offence meant, but me and me mate were wondering what you do for a living," he said to the well-dressed man.

"Oh, no offence taken, friend! I'm a Logical Scientist by profession."

"Oh! What's that then?"

"I'll try to explain by example... Do you have a goldfish at home?"

"Er... mmm... well yeah, I do as it happens!"

"Well, it's logical to follow that you keep it in a bowl or in a pond. Which is it?"

"It's in a pond!"

"Well then it's reasonable to suppose that you have a large garden then?"

"As it happens, yes I have got a big garden!"

"Well then it's logical to assume that in this town if you have large garden then you have a large house?"

"Actually yes, I've got a five bedroom house... built it myself!"

"Well, given that you've built a five bedroom house, it is logical to assume that you haven't built it just for yourself, and that you are quite probably married?"

"Yes I am married, I live with my wife and three children".

"Well then it is logical to assume that you are sexually active with your wife on a regular basis?"

"Damn right, mate! Four nights a week!"

"Well then it is logical to suggest that you do not masturbate very often?"

"Me? Never need to!"

"Well there you are! That's logical science at work – from finding out that you had a goldfish, I've told you about your sex life!"

"I see! That's pretty impressive... thanks mate!"

They both leave the toilet and Dave returns to his mate. "I see the suit was in there. Did you ask him what he does?" Stuart asks Dave.

"Yep! He's a logical scientist!"
"What's that then?"
"I'll try and explain. Do you have a goldfish?"
"Nope."
"Well then, you're a wanker."

WAYS TO HAVE FUN ORDERING A PIZZA

1. If using a touch-tone phone, press random numbers while ordering. Ask the person doing the order to stop doing that.
2. Make up a charge-card name. Ask if they accept it.
3. Use CB codes and lingo at every appropriate opportunity.
4. Order a Big Mac Extra Value meal.
5. Terminate the call with, "Remember, we never had this conversation."
6. Tell the order-taker a rival pizza place is on the other line and you're going with the lowest bidder.
7. Give them your address, then exclaim, "Oh, just surprise me!" and hang up.
8. Answer their questions with questions.
9. In your breathiest voice, tell them to cut the crap about nutrition and ask if they have something outlandishly sinful.
10. Work these bonus phrases in the conversation: ROBUST, ANCIENT EGYPTIAN DEITIES, COST-EFFICIENT, UKRAINIAN, FREE-SPIRITED and PUCE.
11. Tell them to put the crust on top this time.
12. Sing the order to the tune of your favourite song from Metallica's "Master of Puppets" album.
13. Do not name the toppings you want. Instead, spell them out.
14. Stutter on the letter 'p-p-p-p-p-p-P!'.
15. Censored (heh!).
16. Ask for a deal available somewhere else (eg. if phoning Domino's, ask for a Pizza Hut special).
17. Ask what the order taker is wearing.
18. Crack your knuckles into the receiver.
19. Say hello, act stunned for five seconds then behave as if they called you.
20. Rattle off your order with a determined air. If they ask if you would like drinks with that, panic and become disoriented.
21. Tell the order-taker you're depressed. Get him/her to cheer you up.
22. Make a list of exotic cuisines. Order them as toppings.
23. Change your accent every three seconds.
24. Order 52 pepperoni slices prepared in a fractal pattern as

follows from an equation you are about to dictate. Ask if they need paper.

25. Act like you know the order-taker from somewhere. Say "Bed-wetters' Camp, right?"

26. Start your order with, "I'd like..." A little later slap yourself and say, "No, I don't."

27. If they repeat the order to make sure they have it right, say, "OK, that will be 10.99, please pull up to the first window."

28. Declaim all your details and order request in Shakespearean Iambic Pentameter.

29. Order while using an electric knife sharpener.

30. Ask if you get to keep the pizza box. When they say yes, heave a sigh of relief.

31. Put the accent on the last syllable of 'pepperoni'. Use the long "i" sound.

32. Have your pizza "shaken, not stirred".

33. Say, "Are you sure this is Pizza Place?" When they say yes, say, "Well, so is this. You've got some explaining to do!" When they finally offer proof that it is, in fact, Pizza Place, start to cry and ask, "Do you know what it is like to be lied to?"

34. Move the mouthpiece farther and farther from your lips as you speak. When the call ends, jerk the mouthpiece back into place and scream GOODBYE! at the top of your lungs.

35. Tell them to double-check to make sure your pizza is, in fact, dead.

36. Imitate the order-taker's voice.

37. Eliminate all nouns from your speech. Make do with adjectives instead. "You know, the round stuff, meaty, spicy, thinly-cut. Yeah, that's right."

38. When they say, "What would you like?" say, "Huh? Oh you mean now."

39. Play a sitar in the background.

40. Say it's your anniversary and you'd appreciate it if the delivery boy hid behind some furniture waiting for your spouse to arrive so you can surprise him/her.

EVERY SINGLE
ONE OF THESE IS COMPLETELY
AND UTTERLY TRUE

1) Sandwiches taste better cut into two triangles than left as one big square one, but they start going downhill again when cut into four triangles.

2) At the end of every party there is always a girl crying.

3) One of the most awkward things that can happen in a pub is when your pint to toilet cycle gets synchronised with a complete stranger.

4) You've never quite sure whether it's ok to eat green crisps.

5) Everyone who grew up in the 80s has entered the digits 55378008 into a calculator.

6) Reading when you're drunk is horrible.

7) Sharpening a pencil with a knife makes you feel really manly.

8) Your never quite sure whether it's against the law or not to have a fire in your back garden.

9) Nobody ever dares make Cup-a-Soup in a bowl.

10) You never know where to look when eating a banana.

11) Its impossible to describe the smell of a wet cat.

12) Prodding a fire with a stick makes you feel manly.

13) Rummaging in an overgrown garden will always turn up a bouncy ball.

14) You always feel a bit scared when stroking horses.

15) Everyone always remembers the day a dog ran into your school.

16) The most embarrassing thing you can do as schoolchild is to call your teacher mum or dad.

17) The smaller the monkey, the more it looks like it would kill you at the first given opportunity.

18) Some days you see lots of people on crutches.

19) Every bloke has at some stage while taking a pee flushed half way through and then raced against the flush.

20) Old women with mobile phones look wrong!

21) Its impossible to look cool whilst picking up a Frisbee.

22) Driving through a tunnel makes you feel excited.

23) You never ever run out of salt.

24) Old ladies can eat more than you think.

25) You can't respect a man who carries a dog.

26) There's no panic like the panic you momentarily feel when you've got your hand or head stuck in something.

27) No one knows the origins of their metal coat hangers.

28) Despite constant warning, you have never met anybody who has had their arm broken by a swan.

29) The most painful household incident is wearing socks and stepping on an upturned plug.

30) People who don't drive slam car doors too hard.

31) You've turned into your dad the day you put aside a thin piece of wood specifically to stir paint with.

32) Everyone had an uncle who tried to steal their nose.

33) Bricks are horrible to carry.

34) In every plate of chips there is a bad chip.

STRANGERS IN A CUBICLE

Leaving London for Manchester, I decided to make a stop at one of those service stations on the motorway. I went to the WC. The first cubicle was taken so I went to the second one. I'd just sat down when I heard a voice from the next cubicle. "Hi there, how's it going?"

Now I'm not the type to strike up conversations with strangers in WCs at service stations. I didn't know what to say, but finally I said, "...Not bad..."

Then the voice said, "So, what are you doing?"

I thought that was kind of weird, but I said, "Well, I'm just going to the bathroom, then I'm heading back north to Manchester..."

The voice interrupted, "Look, I'm going to have to call you back. Every time I ask you a question, this idiot in the next cubicle keeps answering me!"

TIME OF THE MONTH

A study in Oxford showed that the kind of male face a woman finds attractive may differ depending on where a woman is in her menstrual cycle. For instance, if she is ovulating, she is attracted to men with rugged and masculine features. And if she is menstruating, she is more prone to be attracted to a man with scissors shoved in his temple and a cricket bat jammed up his arse while he is on fire.

DON'T PANIC!
IT'S JUST A FONT!

RUDE SHORTS

He said: "Ever since I first laid eyes on you, I've wanted to make love to you really badly." She said: "Well, you succeeded."

It has been studied and determined that the most often used sexual position for married couples is the doggie position. The husband sits up and begs and the wife rolls over and plays dead.

My husband came home with a tube of KY jelly and said, "This will make you happy tonight." He was right. When he went out of the bedroom, I squirted it all over the doorknobs. He couldn't get back in.

He said: "Two inches more and I would be king." She replied: "Two inches less, and you'd be queen."

WHAT NOT TO DO...

We've all been interviewed for jobs. And we've all spent most of those interviews thinking about what not to do. Don't bite your nails, don't fidget, don't interrupt, don't belch. If we did any of the don'ts, we knew we would disqualify ourselves instantly. But some job applicants go light years beyond this. We surveyed top personnel executives of 100 major American corporations and asked for stories of unusual behaviours by job applicants.

"...stretched out on the floor to fill out the job application."

"She wore a walkman and said she could listen to me and the music at the same time."

"A balding candidate abruptly excused himself. Returned to office a few minutes later, wearing a hairpiece."

"...asked to see interviewer's resume to see if the personnel executive was qualified to judge the candidate."

"...announced she hadn't had lunch and proceeded to eat a hamburger and French fries in the interviewer's office – wiping the ketchup on her sleeve."

"Stated that, if he was hired, he would demonstrate his loyalty by having the corporate logo tattooed on his forearm."

"Interrupted to phone his therapist for advice on answering specific interview questions."

"When I asked him about his hobbies, he stood up and starting tap dancing around my office."

"At the end of the interview, while I stood there dumbstruck, he went through my purse, took out my brush, then brushed his hair and left."

"...pulled out a Polaroid camera and snapped a flash picture of me. Said he collected photos of everyone who interviewed him."

"Said he wasn't interested because the position paid too much."

"While I was on a long-distance phone call, the applicant took out a copy of Penthouse and looked through the photos only, stopping longest at the centerfold."

"During the interview, an alarm clock went off from the candidate's brief case. He took it out, shut it off, apologized and said he had to leave for another interview."

"A telephone call came in for the job applicant. It was from his wife. His side of the conversation went like this: 'Which company? When do I start? What's the salary?' I said, 'I assume you're not interested in conducting the interview any further.' He promptly responded, 'I am as long as you'll pay me more.' I didn't hire him, but later found out that there was no other job offer. It was a scam to get a higher offer."

"His brief case opened when he picked it up and the contents spilled, revealing ladies' undergarments and assorted make up and perfume."

"Candidate said he really didn't want to get a job, but the unemployment office needed proof that he was looking for one."

"...asked who the lovely babe was, pointing to the picture on my desk. When I said it was my wife, he asked if she was home now and wanted my phone number. I called security."

"Pointing to a black case he carried into my office, he said that if he was not hired, the bomb would go off. Astounded, I began to state why he would never be hired and that I was going to call the police. He then reached down to the case, flipped a switch and ran. No one was injured but I did need to get a new desk."

THE INFLATABLE JOKE

An inflatable pupil goes to his inflatable school and is having a really bad day. Bored in his history lesson he gets up and walks out. Walking down the corridor he sees the inflatable headmaster walking towards him, and he pulls a knife out and stabs him. He runs out of the school. As he gets outside he thinks again "I hate school," and pulls his knife out and stabs the inflatable school. He runs off to his inflatable home. Two hours later his inflatable Mum is knocking at his inflatable bedroom door with the inflatable police. Panicking, the inflatable boy pulls out the knife and stabs himself.

Later on in the evening he wakes up in the inflatable hospital and sees the inflatable headmaster is in the inflatable bed next to him. Shaking his deflated head more in sorrow than in anger, the inflatable headmaster gravely intones, "I'm disappointed in you, boy. You've let me down, you've let the school down, but worst of all, you've let yourself down."

ESSEX GIRLS – NEW JOKES

An Essex girl walks into the local dry cleaners. She places a garment on the counter. "I'll be back tomorrow afternoon to pick up my dress," she says. "Come again?" says the clerk, cupping his ear. "Yeah," she replies. "And this time there's some mayonnaise, too."

An Essex Girl enters a sex shop and asks for a vibrator. The man says, "Choose from our range on the wall." She says, "I'll take the red one."

The man replies, "You can't, that's a fire extinguisher."

Another Essex girl was involved in a serious crash. There was blood everywhere. The paramedics arrived and dragged the girl out of the now-burning car so that she was lying flat out on the floor. "Right," said the Paramedic, "I'm going to check if you're concussed. How many fingers am I putting up, Sharon?" The Essex Girl went pale. "Oh my God I'm paralysed from the waist down!"

An Essex girl and an Irish guy are in a bar when the Essex girl notices something strange about the wellies the Irish guy is wearing. She says, "Scuse me mate, I ain't being funny or nuffink, but why az one of your wellies 'ave an L on it and the uva one's got an R on it." So the Irish guy smiles, puts down his glass of Guinness and replies, "Well lass, Oi'm a little bit thick, ye see. The one with the R on it is for me right foot and the one with the L is for me left foot." "Cor blimey, exclaims the Essex girl, "So THAT'S why me knickers got C&A on 'em."

DRIVING TO THE CASHPOINT MACHINE.

HIM:
1) Drive up to the vicinity of the cash point and park safely.
2) Walk to the cash point.
3) Insert card.
4) Enter PIN number and amount.
5) Take cash, card and receipt.

HER:
1) Pull up on the zigzags or a double yellow line, with hazard lights on.
2) Check make-up.
3) Turn off engine, put on handbrake.
4) Put keys in handbag.
5) Get out of car, adjust hair.
6) Get keys back out of handbag, lock car, put keys back in handbag.

7) Get to the front of the queue for the cash point, then open handbag and remove purse.

8) Now start looking for the card.

9) Insert card.

10) Now insert the right card.

11) Hunt in handbag for tampon wrapper with PIN number written on it.

12) Enter PIN number.

13) Study instructions for at least two minutes.

14) Hit 'cancel'.

15) Re-enter correct PIN number.

16) Hit 'cancel'.

17) Search in handbag for mobile phone.

18) Call husband or boyfriend to get correct PIN number.

19) Do not step aside to let anyone else 'in' ahead of you.

20) Re-enter correct PIN number.

21) Check balance.

22) Look for envelope.

23) Look in purse for pen.

24) Make out deposit slip.

25) Endorse cheques.

26) Make deposit.

27) Study instructions.

28) Order a statement.

29) Order a new chequebook.

30) Enter amount.

31) Re-enter 70, not 700.

32) Count cash while still stood right in front of the cash point.

33) Put cash in purse.

34) Put purse in handbag.

35) Leave vicinity of the cash point, which now has an 8-person queue.

36) Look for keys in handbag.

37) Unlock and get into car.

38) Check make-up.

39) Look for keys in handbag.

40) Start car.

41) Check hair in rear-view mirror.

42) Re-adjust rear-view mirror to its normal position.

43) Pull away without looking in rear-view mirror.

44) STOP.

45) Reverse back up to the parking space on the zigzags or

double yellow lines.
46) Shut off the engine.
47) Put keys in handbag.
48) Get out of car, adjust hair.
49) Get keys back out of handbag.
50) Lock car.
51) Go back to the cash point.
52) Jump in front of everyone and take your card and receipt.
53) Look for keys in handbag.
54) Unlock and get back in the car.
55) Put card in purse.
56) Put receipt in chequebook.
57) Search for pen in handbag.
58) Enter deposits and withdrawals in chequebook.
59) Make space in handbag for purse and chequebook.
60) Close handbag and place on floor.
61) Look for keys.
62) Pick up handbag from floor, and get the keys.
63) Switch on ignition.
64) Check make-up.
65) Check hair in rear-view mirror.
66) Re-adjust rear-view mirror to its normal position.
67) Put car in gear, reverse.
68) Put gear in first.
69) Switch on ignition again after stalling.
70) Pull away without looking in rear-view mirror.
71) Wave to the bloke behind you who's just had someone smack him up the arse.
72) Continue to drive for next three miles.
73) Turn off hazard lights.
74) Take off hand-brake.

NOW THAT IS A
LAME EXCUSE

A wife and her husband were having a dinner party for some important guests. The wife was very excited about this and wanted everything to be perfect. At the very last minute, she realized that she didn't have any snails for the dinner party, so she asked her husband to run down to the beach with the bucket to gather some snails. Very grudgingly he agreed. He took the bucket, walked out the door, down the steps and out to the park.

As he was collecting the snails, he noticed a beautiful woman strolling alongside the path. He kept thinking to himself, "Wouldn't it be great if she would even just come down and talk to me?" He went back to gathering the snails. All of a sudden he looked up and the beautiful woman was standing right over him. They started talking and she invited him back to her place. They ended up spending the night together.

At seven o'clock the next morning he woke up and exclaimed, "Oh no! My wife's dinner party!" He gathered all his clothes, put them on real fast, grabbed his bucket and ran out the door. He ran from the park all the way to his first floor apartment. He was in such a hurry that when he got to the top of the stairs, he dropped the bucket of snails. There were snails all down the stairs.

The door opened just then, with a very angry wife standing in the doorway, wondering where he'd been all this time. He looked at the snails all down the steps, then he looked at her, then back at the snails and said, "Come on guys, we're almost there!"

WHO WAS THIS JESUS PERSON ANYWAY...

There are three good arguments that Jesus was black:
1. He called everyone "brother"
2. He liked gospel.
3. He couldn't get a fair trial.

There are three equally good arguments that Jesus was Jewish:
1. He went into his father's business.
2. He lived at home until he was 33.
3. He was sure his mother was a virgin and his mother was sure he was God.

There are also three equally good arguments that Jesus was Italian:
1. He talked with his hands.
2. He had wine with every meal.
3. He used olive oil.

And then there are three equally good arguments that Jesus was a Californian:
1. He never cut his hair.
2. He walked around barefoot all the time.
3. He started a new religion.

There are also three equally good arguments that Jesus was Irish:
1. He never got married.
2. He was always telling stories.
3. He loved green pastures.

But the most compelling evidence of all – three arguments that Jesus was a woman:
1. He fed a crowd at a moment's notice when there was no food.
2. He kept trying to get a message across to a bunch of men who just didn't get it.
3. And even when he was dead, he had to get up because there was more work to do.

IMAGINE IF ALL MAJOR RETAILERS STARTED MAKING THEIR OWN CONDOMS AND KEPT THE SAME TAGLINE...

Sainsbury – Making life taste better

Tesco – Every little helps

Nike – Just do it

Peugeot – The ride of your life

Galaxy – Why have rubber when you can have silk

KFC – Finger-licking good

Minstrels – Melts in your mouth, not in your hands

Safeway – Lightening the load

Abbey National – Because life is complicated enough

Coca-Cola – The real thing

Duracell – Keeps on going and going

Pringles – Once you pop, you can't stop

Burger king – Home of the Whopper

Goodyear – For a longer ride, go wide

Muller light – So much pleasure, but where's the pain

Flash – Just sit back, relax and let Flash do all the hard work

Halfords – We go the extra mile

Royal Mail – I saw this and thought of you

Andrex – Soft, strong and very, very long

Renault – Size really does matter

Ronseal – Does exactly what is says on the tin

Domestos – Gets right under the rim

Heineken – Reaches parts that other condoms cannot reach

Carlsberg – Probably the best condom in the world

AA – For the 4th emergency service

Pepperami – It's a bit of an animal

Polo – The condom with the hole (VERY poor seller!)

FREE CHEESE FRIDAY™

LAST WORDS

Mary Clancy goes up to Father O'Grady after his Sunday morning service, and she's in tears. He says, "So what's bothering you, Mary my dear?"

She says, "Oh, Father, I've got terrible news. My husband passed away last night."

The priest says, "Oh, Mary, that's terrible. Tell me, Mary, did he have any last requests?"

She says, "That he did, Father."

The priest says, "What did he ask, Mary?"

She says, "He said, 'Please Mary, put down that damn gun...'"

PLAYING WITH FIRE
(MESSING WITH BLONDES)

A blind man enters a Ladies Bar by mistake. He finds his way to a bar stool and orders a drink. After sitting there for a while, he yells to the bartender, "Hey, you wanna hear a blonde joke?"

The bar immediately falls absolutely quiet. In a very deep, husky voice, the woman next to him says, "Before you tell that joke, sir, you should know five important things: First, the bartender is a blonde woman. Second, the bouncer is a blonde woman. Third, I'm a 6 feet tall, 200 pound blonde woman with a black belt in karate. Fourth, the woman sitting next to me is also a blonde, and she is a professional weightlifter. Fifth, the lady to your right is a blonde and is a professional wrestler. Now think about it seriously, Mister. Do you still wanna tell that joke?"

The blind man thinks for a second, shakes his head and declares, "Nah. Not if I'm gonna have to explain it five times."

A BIT OF COOKIE

A man enters the confessional and says, "Father, it has been one month since my last confession. I have had sex with Cookie Green every week for the last month."

The priest tells the sinner, "You are forgiven. Go out and say three Hail Marys"

Soon, another man enters the confessional. "Father, it has been two months since my last confession. I have had sex with Cookie Green twice a week for the last two months."

This time the priest asks, "Who is Cookie Green?"

"A new woman in the neighbourhood," the sinner replies.

"Very well," says the priest. "Go and say ten Hail Marys."

The next morning in church the priest is preparing to deliver his sermon, when suddenly a gorgeous, tall woman enters. All the men's eyes fall upon her, as she slowly sashays up the aisle and sits down right in front of the priest. Her dress is green and very short, with matching shiny emerald green shoes. The priest and altar boy gasp, as the woman in the matching green shoes and dress sits with her legs slightly spread apart. The priest turns to the altar boy and asks, "Is that Cookie Green?"

The altar boy, whose eyes are popping out of his head, replies, "No, I think it's just the reflection off her shoes..."

THE TALKING HORSE

This geezer is sitting reading his newspaper when the wife sneaks up behind him and whacks him on the head with a frying pan. "What was that for?" he says.

"That was for the piece of paper in your trouser pocket with the name Mary-Ellen written on it," she replies.

"Don't be daft," he explains, "two weeks ago when I went to the races, Mary-Ellen was the name of one of the horses I bet on."

She seems satisfied at this and apologises and goes off to do work around the house. Three days later he's again sitting in his chair reading when she nails him with an even bigger frying pan, knocking him out cold. When he comes around, he says, "What the hell was that for?"

"Your f**king horse phoned!"

AUSTRALIAN NEWSFLASH...

Hot off the wire from the Australian Medical Association: Australian Medical Association researchers have made a remarkable discovery. It seems that some patients needing blood transfusions may benefit from receiving chicken blood rather than human blood. It tends to make the men more cocky, and the women lay better.

DUBYA

One night, George W. Bush is awakened in the White House by the ghost of George Washington. Now worrying about how history will remember him, George W. (a.k.a. "Dubya") asks the ghost, "Mr. Washington, sir, what is the best thing I can do to help the American people so I'm remembered more better?"

"Set an honest and honourable example, George, just as I did," replies George Washington.

The following evening, the ghost of Thomas Jefferson appears before Bush in the dark bedroom. "Mr. Jefferson, sir," George W. asks again, "what is the best thing I can do to help the American people so I'm remembered more better?"

"Preserve the land for future generations, and stay out of foreign affairs," replies Jefferson.

Bush isn't sleeping well the next night and sees yet another figure moving in the shadows. It's the ghost of Abraham Lincoln. "Mr. Lincoln, sir, what is the best thing I can do to help the American people so I'm remembered more better?" George asks.

Lincoln's ghostly eyes glitter. "Go see a play."

UNDERSTANDING
THE IT GUY – TAKE ONE

Two IT guys were walking across the park one day, when they spotted a colleague riding a brand new bike. "Where did you get such a great bike?" they marvelled.

The third guy replied, "Well, I was walking along yesterday minding my own business when a beautiful woman rode up on this bike. She threw the bike to the ground, took off all her clothes and said, 'Take what you want, big boy!'"

The first IT guy nodded approvingly, "Good choice. The clothes probably wouldn't have fit."

UNDERSTANDING THE IT GUY — TAKE TWO

An architect, an artist and an IT guy were discussing whether it was better to have a wife or a mistress. The architect said he enjoyed his time with his wife, building a solid foundation for an enduring relationship. The artist said he enjoyed time with his mistress, because of the passion and mystery he found there. The IT guy said, "I like both."

The artist said "Both? Isn't that a bit excessive?"

The IT guy replied "Yeah, but if you have a wife and a mistress, they will each assume you are spending time with the other woman, so you can sneak off to the office and get some work done."

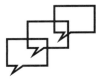

UNDERSTANDING THE IT GUY — TAKE THREE:

To the optimist, the glass is half full.
To the pessimist, the glass is half empty.
To the IT guy, the glass is twice as big as it needs to be.

SEX AT HOME

An Italian, a Frenchman and an Irishman are discussing love-making techniques, and all are showing off. The Italian says, "When I have a-finished makina love with my girl-a-friend, I go down and gently tickle the back of her knees. She floatsa SIX inches abova da bed in ecstasy."

The Frenchman replies, "Zat is nothing, when ah áve finished making ze love with ze girlfriend ah kiss all ze way down her body and zen ah lick ze soles of her feet wiz mah tongue and she floats TWELVE inches above ze bed in pure ecstasy."

The Irishman says, "Dat's nottin'. When oi've finished shaggin' me bord, I get out of da bed, walk over to d'window and wipe me knob on the curtains. She hits the fockin' roof..."

THE HIPPOCRATIC OAF

Doctor Dave had slept with one of his patients and had felt guilty all day long. No matter how much he tried to forget about it, he couldn't. The guilt and sense of betrayal was overwhelming. But every once in a while he'd hear that soothing voice within himself, trying to reassure him, "Dave, don't worry about it. You aren't the first doctor to sleep with one of their patients and you won't be the last. And you're single. Let it go..." But invariably the other voice inside his head would bring him back to reality: "Dave, you're a vet..."

HOW TO TURN A COP INTO A VEGETABLE...

"Is there a problem, Officer?" "Ma'am, you were speeding."

"Oh, I see."

"Can I see your license please?"

"I'd give it to you but I don't have one."

"Don't have one?"

"Lost it four times for drunk driving."

"I see... Can I see your vehicle registration papers please."

"I can't do that."

"Why not?"

"I stole this car."

"Stole it?"

"Yes, and I killed and hacked up the owner."

"You what?"

"His body parts are in plastic bags in the trunk if you want to see."

The officer looks at the woman and slowly backs away to his car and calls for backup. Within minutes five police cars circle the woman and a senior officer slowly approaches the car, clasping his half-drawn gun.

"Ma'am, could you step out of your vehicle please!" asks the senior officer.

She gets out slowly, saying, "Is there a problem sir?"

"My colleague told me that you stole this car and murdered the owner."

"Murdered the owner?"

"Yes. Could you open the trunk of your car, please?"

The woman opens the trunk, revealing nothing but an empty trunk.

"Is this your car, ma'am?"

"Yes, here are the registration papers."

The officer is quite stunned. "My colleague claimed that you do not have a driver's license." The woman digs into her handbag and carefully pulls out a clutch purse and hands it to the officer. He snaps open the clutch purse and examines the license. He looks quite puzzled. "I must admit, ma'am, that I'm confused. The officer told me you didn't have a license, that you stole this car and that you murdered the owner."

"I suppose the lying bastard told you I was speeding, too?"

I TAKE OFFENCE
TO THIS ONE, PEOPLE...

The only seat available on the train was directly adjacent to a well-dressed middle-aged French woman, but the seat was being used by her dog. The weary traveller asked, "Ma'am, please move your dog. I need that seat."

The French woman looked down her nose at the American, sniffed and said, "You Americans. Your are such a rude class of people. Can't you see my little Fifi is using that seat?"

The American walked away, determined to find a place to rest, but after another trip down to the end of the train, found himself again facing the woman with the do again. One more he asked, "Please, lady. May I sit there? I'm very tired."

The French woman wrinkled her nose and snorted "You Americans! Not only are you rude, you are also arrogant... Imagine!"

The American didn't say anything else. He leaned over, picked up the dog, tossed it out the window of the train and sat down in the empty seat. The woman shrieked and railed and demanded that someone defend her honour and chastise the American.

An Englishman sitting across the aisle spoke up indignantly. "You know, sir, you Americans do seem to have a penchant for doing the wrong thing. You eat holding the fork in the wrong hand. You drive your cars on the wrong side of the road. And now, Sir, you've thrown the wrong bitch out of the window."

PRAYERS

The Lord's prayer for women:
Our Marks, Which art with Spencer's
Hallowed be thy food hall.
Thy Gucci watch, Thy Kookaï bag
In Hermès As it is in Harrods.
Give us each day our Visa Gold,
And forgive us our overdraft,
As we forgive those who stop our Next card,
And lead us not into Dorothy Perkins,
But deliver us from Top Shop,
For thine is the Prada, the Cartier and the Versace,
For Gaultier and Eternity, Amex.
The Lord's prayer for blokes:
Our beer, Which art in barrels,
Hallowed be thy drink.
Thy will be drunk, I will be drunk,
At home as it is in the local.
Forgive us this day our daily spillage,
And lead us not into the practice
Of poncey wine tasting,
And deliver us from alcopops,
For mine is the bitter, the ale and the lager,
Forever and ever, Barmen.

A CASE OF I TOLD YOU SO...

This is a story about a couple who had been happily married for years.
The only friction in their marriage was the husband's habit of farting
loudly every morning when he awoke. The noise would wake his wife
and the smell would make her eyes water and make her gasp for air.
Every morning she would plead with him to stop ripping them off be-

cause it was making her sick. He told her he couldn't stop it and that it was perfectly natural. She told him to see a doctor; she was concerned that one day he would blow his guts out. The years went by and he continued to rip them out.

Then one Thanksgiving morning as she was preparing the turkey for dinner and he was upstairs sound asleep, she looked at the bowl where she had put the turkey innards and neck, gizzard, liver and all the spare parts and a malicious thought came to her. She took the bowl and went upstairs where her husband was sound asleep and, gently pulling back the bed covers, she pulled back the elastic waistband of his underpants and emptied the bowl of turkey guts into his shorts. Some time later she heard her husband waken with his usual trumpeting which was followed by a blood curdling scream and the sound of frantic footsteps as he ran into the bathroom.

The wife could hardly control herself as she rolled on the floor laughing, tears in her eyes! After years of torture she reckoned she had got him back pretty good. About 20 minutes later, her husband came downstairs in his bloodstained underpants with a look of horror on his face. She bit her lip as she asked him what was the matter.

He said, "Honey, you were right. All these years you have warned me and I didn't listen to you."

"What do you mean?" asked his wife.

"Well, you always told me that someday I would end up farting my guts out and today it finally happened. But by the grace of God, some Vaseline and these two fingers, I think I got most of them back in."

RANDOM THOUGHTS

Insanity is my only means of relaxation.
I gave up jogging for my health because my thighs kept rubbing together and setting my knickers on fire.
Amazing! You hang something in your closet for a while and it shrinks two sizes!

£££££££££££

POUND PUZZLE

Think about this one...

Three students need to buy a TV. They see one for 15 pounds and spend a fiver each. The shopkeeper is feeling generous, so he sends his assistant after them to give them a fiver back, in the form of five pound coins.

On the way there the assistant decides it would be easier all round if he gave them three coins to divide between them and kept two pounds for himself.

In the end:

The students are happy to have spend only four pounds each (12 pounds in total).

The assistant has two pounds in his pocket.

So what happened to the missing pound coin?

Answer:
You should be counting down from £15, not up from £10. The two pounds the assistant has are the cash from the student's £12 to the shopkeeper's £10, not from the £12 to the £15 already paid.

FUNNY, THE SAME THING HAPPENED WITH MY WIFE... ??

A mild-mannered man was tired of being bossed around by his wife, so he went to a psychiatrist. The psychiatrist said he needed to build his self-esteem and gave him a book on assertiveness, which he read on the way home. Rendered bold by what he had read, the man stormed into the house and walked up to his wife.

Pointing a finger in her face, he said, "From now on, I want you to know that I am the man of this house and my word is law! I want you to prepare me a gourmet meal tonight and when I'm finished eating my meal, I expect a sumptuous dessert afterward. Then, after dinner, you're going to draw me my bath so I can relax. And when I'm finished with my bath, guess who's going to dress me and comb my hair?"
"The funeral director!" said his wife.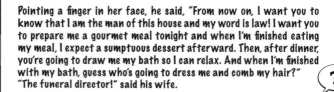

The Frenchman replies, "Zat is nothing, when ah 'ave finished making ze love with ze girlfriend ah kiss all ze way down her body and zen ah lick ze soles of her feet wiz mah tongue and she floats TWELVE inches above ze bed in pure ecstasy."

The Irishman says, "Dat's nottin'. When oi've finished shaggin' me bord, I get out of da bed, walk over to d'window and wipe me knob on the curtains. She hits the fockin' roof..."

I LIKE SHORT SHORTS!!

A severed penis has been found in a back garden in Houston, Texas. Police believe it to be a shuttlecock.

My wife asked me to kiss her where it's smelly! So I took her to Blackpool.

Two prostitutes are standing on a street corner. One says to the other, "Have you ever been picked up by the fuzz?" The other replies, "No, but I've been swung around by the tits."

Q: Name three football clubs that contain swear words? A: ARSEnal, sCUNThorpe and Fucking West Ham!!

MEET THE PARENTS

A girl asks her boyfriend to come over Friday night and have dinner with her parents. Since this is such a big event, the girl announced to her boyfriend that after dinner, she would like to go out and make love for the first time. Well, the boy is ecstatic, but he has never had sex before, so he takes a trip to the pharmacist to get some condoms.

The pharmacist helps the boy for about an hour. He tells the boy everything there is to know about condoms and sex. At the counter, the pharmacist asks the boy how many condoms he'd like to buy, a 3-pack, 10-pack, or a family pack.

"I'm really going to give it to this girl," the boy tells the pharmacist. "I intend to plug every orifice in her body at least twice."

The pharmacist, with a laugh, suggests the family pack, saying the boy will be rather busy, it being his first time and all. That night, the boy shows up at the girl's parents house and meets his girlfriend at the door. "Oh I'm so excited for you to meet my parents, come on in!"

The boy goes inside and is taken to the dinner table where the girl's parents are seated. The boy quickly offers to say grace and bows his head. He says grace, and everyone else starts eating, but a minute passes, and the boy is still deep in prayer with his head down. 10 minutes passes and still no movement from the boy. Finally, after 20 minutes with his head down, the girlfriend finally leans over and whispers to the boyfriend, "I had no idea you were this religious."

The boy turns and whispers back, "I had no idea your father was a pharmacist."

CUTE AND CUDDLY

A woman meets a gorgeous man in a bar. They talk, they connect, they end up leaving together. They get back to his place and as he shows her around his apartment, she notices that his bedroom is completely packed with sweet cuddly teddy bears. Hundreds of cute little bears are ranged all the way along the floor. There are loads of cuddly medium sized ones on a shelf a little higher, and a number of huge enormous bears on the top shelf, reaching up almost to the ceiling.

The woman is a bit surprised that a man would have such a collection of teddy bears, especially one so extensive, but she decides not to mention this to him and is actually quite impressed that he can so freely express his sensitive side. She turns to him, they kiss and then they rip each other's clothes off and make hot steamy love.

After an intense night of passion with this sensitive man, lying together in the afterglow, the woman leans in to him and whispers, "How was it for you, darling?"
The man says, "Not bad, actually. Help yourself to any prize from the lower shelf."

SORTED WITH THE MISSUS

"Doc, I can't stop singing 'The green, green grass of home'." "That sounds like Tom Jones syndrome." "Is it common?" "It's not unusual."

Two cows are standing next to each other in a field. Daisy says to Dolly, "I was artificially inseminated this morning." "I don't believe you," says Dolly. "It's true, says Daisy. "Straight up, no bull!"

A guy walks into the psychiatrist wearing only cling film for shorts. The shrink says, "Well, I can clearly see you're nuts."

Two hydrogen atoms walk into a bar. One says, "I think I've lost an electron." The other says, "Are you sure?" "Yes, I'm positive..."
Answer phone message "If you want to buy marijuana, press the hash key..."

BRIGHTNESS TEST — FAILED

While visiting England, George Bush is invited to tea with the Queen. He asks her what her leadership philosophy is. She says that it is to surround herself with intelligent people. He asks how she knows if they're intelligent. "I do so by asking them the right questions," says the Queen. "Allow me to demonstrate."

She phones Tony Blair (using a speaker phone) and says, "Mr. Prime Minister, please answer this question, 'Your mother has a child and your father has a child and this child is not your brother or sister. Who is it?'"

Tony Blair responds, "It's me, ma'am."

"Correct. Thank you and good-bye, sir," says the Queen. She hangs up and says, "Did you get that, Mr. Bush?"

"Yes ma'am. Thanks a lot. I'll definitely be using that!"

Upon returning to Washington, he decides he'd better put the Chairman of the Senate Foreign Relations Committee to the test. He summons Jesse Helms to the White House and says, "Senator Helms, I wonder if you'd mind answering a question for me?"

"Why, of course, sir. What's on your mind?"

"Uhh, your mother has a child and your father has a child and this child is not your brother or your sister. Who is it?" Helms hems and haws and finally asks, "Can I think about it and get back to you?"

Bush agrees and Helms leaves. Helms immediately calls a meeting of other senior Republican senators and they puzzle over the question for several hours, but nobody can come up with an answer. Finally, in desperation, Helms calls Colin Powell at the State Department and explains his problem. "Now look here, son, your mother has a child and your father has a child and this child is not your brother or your sister. Who is it?"

Powell answers immediately, "It's me of course, you damn idiot."

Much relieved, Helms rushes back to the White House and exclaims, "I know the answer, sir! I know who it is! It's Colin Powell!"

Shaking his head in disgust, Bush replies, "Wrong, Senator. It's Tony Blair."

LOVING HUBBIES ET AL

An elderly gent was invited to his old friend's home for dinner one evening. He was impressed by the way his buddy preceded every request to his wife with endearing terms: Honey, My Love, Darling, Sweetheart, Pumpkin, etc. The couple had been married almost 70 years and clearly, they were still very much in love.

While his wife was in the kitchen, the man leaned over and said to his host, "I think it's wonderful that, after all these years, you still call your wife those loving pet names."

The old man hung his head. "To be honest with you," he said, "I forgot her name about 10 years ago."

RSPCA

A man hated his wife's cat and he decided to get rid of it. He drove two blocks away from home and dropped the cat there. When he got back home, the cat was already walking up the driveway . The next day, he decided to drop the cat four blocks away but the same thing happened. He kept on increasing the number of blocks but the cat kept on coming home before him.

At last, he decided to drive a few miles away, turn right, then turn left, past the bridge, then right again and another right and so on until he reached what he thought was a perfect spot and dropped the cat there. Hours later, the man called his wife at home and asked her, "Is the cat there?"

"Yes, why do you ask?" answered the wife.

Frustrated, the man said, "Put that cat on the phone, I'm lost and I need directions."

COME-UPPANCE

An Australian man was having coffee and croissants with butter and jam in a cafe when an American tourist, chewing gum, sat down next to him. The Australian politely ignored the American, who, nevertheless, started up a conversation.

The American snapped his gum and said, "You Australian folk eat the whole bread?"

The Australian frowned, annoyed with being bothered during his breakfast and replied, "Of course."

The American blew a huge bubble. "We don't. In the States, we only eat what's inside. The crusts we collect in a container, recycle them, transform them into croissants and sell them to Australia."

The American had a smirk on his face. The Australian listened in silence. The American persisted. "D'ya eat jam with the bread?"

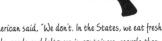

Sighing, the Australian replied, "Of course."

Cracking his gum between his teeth, the American said, "We don't. In the States, we eat fresh fruit for breakfast, then we put all the peels, seeds and leftovers in containers, recycle them, transform them into jam and sell it to Australia."

The Australian then asked, "Do you have sex in the States?"

The American smiled and said, "Why of course we do."

The Australian leaned closer to him and asked, "And what do you do with the condoms once you've used them?"

"We throw them away, of course."

"We don't. In Australia, we put them in a container, recycle them, transform them into chewing gum and sell it to the United States." He paused for a moment. "Why do you think it's called Wrigley's?"

YOU IN YOUR VW...

The other day I was cruising along as usual in my BMW, coming onto one of MY motorways, which was very busy with inferior cars. First off, I couldn't believe that the volume of traffic DIDN'T slow down for me AT ALL as I came off the slip road! I had to squeeze into a barely big enough gap between two cars in order to get onto my motorway! (The driver of the car behind me did realise his mistake though and honked an apology to me with a long blast of his horn.) Unbelievably, I had to do the same again before I could get to the BMW lane. Why do underlings use this lane? Surely everyone knows it is for BMW drivers only?

Anyway, once I was in the BMW lane and posing along at 110mph enjoying the adulation that the inferior car drivers were giving me, I noticed an inferior car ahead of me which was not only in the BMW lane of my motorway, but was driving at a ridiculous 70 mph! Naturally, I got to within a foot or so of his rear bumper and flashed my headlights to remind him he shouldn't be in the BMW lane of my motorway and to get out of my way. Of course, once he realised it was a BMW behind him, he did just that, but I could hardly believe it when he pulled straight back out behind me! He also tried to keep up with me and when he realised I would out-run him, he put on some blue lights in his front grill and urged me to get onto the hard shoulder so that he could congratulate me on my excellent car.

Needless to say, I was eager to oblige and when we had stopped, the man gave me a piece of paper confirming what I already knew – that my car goes fast! Apparently he wants everyone to know what a superior car I have, so I had to take my driver's licence to a Police Station to be sent away to have some points put on! They're not free points either – they're £20 each and I was only allowed three. But the man at the Police Station said that because I drive a BMW, it won't be much longer before I earn the full 12 points, and then I won't even NEED a driving licence, so they will take it off me! See, now THAT's the sort of respect you get when you drive a BMW.

FIVE SECRETS TO A GREAT RELATIONSHIP

1. It is important to find a man who works around the house, occasion-ally cooks and cleans, and who has a job.
2. It is important to find a man who makes you laugh.
3. It is important to find a man who is dependable and doesn't lie.
4. It is important to find a man who's good in bed and who loves to have sex with you.
5. It is important that these four men never meet.

HAHAHA

Into a Belfast pub comes Paddy Murphy, looking like he'd just been run over by a train. His arm is in a sling, his nose is broken, his face is cut and bruised and he's walking with a limp. "What happened to you?" asks Sean, the bartender.

"Jamie O'Connor and me had a fight," says Paddy.

"That little shit, O'Connor," says Sean, "He couldn't do that to you, he must have had something in his hand."

"That he did," says Paddy. "A shovel is what he had, and a terrible lickin' he gave me with it."

"Well," says Sean, "you should have defended yourself, didn't you have something in your hand?"

"That I did," said Paddy. "Mrs. O'Connor's breast, and for sure a thing of beauty it was, but not all that useful in a fight."

A CASE OF MISTAKEN IDENTITY

Three Irishmen, Paddy, Sean and Shamus, were stumbling home from the pub late one night and found themselves on the road which led past the old graveyard. "Come have a look over here," says Paddy, "It's Michael O'Grady's grave, God bless his soul. He lived to the ripe old age of 87."

"That's nothing", says Sean, "here's one named Patrick O' Tool, it says here that he was 95 when he died."
Just then, Shamus yells out, "Good God, here's a fella that got to be 145!"

"What was his name?" asks Paddy.

Shamus stumbles around a bit, awkwardly lights a match to see what else is written on the stone marker and exclaims, "Miles, from Dublin."

THE STUPID TEST!

OK. Pay close attention. Here is a very simple little test comprising of four easy questions to determine the level of your intellect. See if you have what it takes to be considered "smart". Your replies must be spontaneous and immediate, with no deliberating or wasting of time. And no cheating!

On your marks, get set, go...

1: You are competing in a race and overtake the runner in second place. In which position are you now?

2: If you overtake the last runner, what position are you now in?

3: Take 1,000. Add 40. Add another 1,000. Add 30. 1,000 again. Plus 20. Plus 1,000. And plus 10. What is the total?

4: Marie's father has five daughters: 1. Chacha 2. Cheche 3. Chichi 4. Chocho 5. ???? What is the fifth daughter's name?

Answers:

1: If you answered that you're now in first, you're wrong! You overtook the second runner and took his place, therefore you are now in second place.

2: If you answered second to last, or last, you are wrong once again. Think about it... How can you overtake the person who is last? If you're behind them, they can't be last unless the race is on a circuit and you're lapping them. So first is a better guess, but it's still wrong, I'm afraid – the only correct answer is that you can't tell, because you can theoretically lap last place from any position (other, obviously, than last!).

3: Answer: 5,000? Wrong again! The correct answer is 4,100. Try again with a good calculator.

4: Answer: Chuchu? Wrong, you have been blinded by the pattern... It's obviously Marie! Read the question properly.

SOMETHING TO THINK ABOUT ON YOUR NEXT DREAM VACATION!!!

The average blue whale produces over 400 gallons of sperm when it ejaculates, but only 10% of that actually makes it into his mate. So 360 gallons are spilled into the ocean every time one unloads – and you wonder why the ocean is so salty...

RANDOM RANTS

- Give a person a fish and you feed them for a day. Teach that person to use the Internet and they won't bother you for weeks.

- How is it one careless match can start a forest fire, but it takes a whole box to start a campfire?

- Health nuts are going to feel stupid someday... lying in hospitals, dying of nothing.

- The other night I ate at a real family restaurant. Every table had an argument going.

- Have you noticed since everyone has a camera phone and/or a camcorder these days, suddenly we seem to be having a rash of UFO sightings?

- According to a recent survey, men say the first thing that they notice about a woman is her eyes, and women say the first thing they notice about men is that they're a bunch of liars.

- Whenever I feel blue, I start breathing again.

- All of us could take a lesson from the weather. It pays no attention to criticism.

- Have you noticed that a slight tax increase costs you two hundred pounds and a substantial tax cut saves you twenty pence?

- In the 60s people took acid to make the world weird. Now the world is weird and people take Prozac to make it normal.

- Politics is supposed to be the second oldest profession. I have come to realize that it bears a very close resemblance to the first.

- There is a theory which states that if ever anybody discovers exactly what the Universe is for and why it is here, it will instantly disappear and be replaced by something even more bizarre and inexplicable. There is another theory which states that this has already happened. A lot.

- I read recipes the same way I read science fiction. I get to the end and I think, "Well, that's not going to happen."

23 THINGS YOU SHOULD KNOW

1. If you're too open-minded, your brains will fall out.
2. Age is a very high price to pay for maturity.
3. Going to church doesn't make you a Christian, any more than standing in a garage makes you a car.
4. Artificial intelligence is no match for natural stupidity.
5. If you must choose between two evils, pick the one you've never tried before.
6. My idea of housework is to sweep the room with a glance.
7. Not one shred of evidence supports the notion that life is serious.
8. It is easier to get forgiveness than permission.
9. For every action, there is an equal and opposite government program.
10. If you look like your passport picture, you probably need the trip.

11. Bills travel through the mail at twice the speed of checks.

12. A conscience is what hurts when all of your other parts feel so good.

13. Eat well, stay fit, die anyway.

14. Men are from earth. Women are from earth. Deal with it.

15. No man has ever been shot while doing the dishes.

16. A balanced diet is a cookie in each hand.

17. Middle age is when broadness of the mind and narrowness of the waist change places.

18. Opportunities always look bigger going than coming.

19. Junk is something you've kept for years and throw away three weeks before you need it.

20. There is always one more imbecile than you counted on.

21. Experience is a wonderful thing. It enables you to recognize a mistake when you make it again.

22. By the time you can make ends meet, they move the ends.

23. Someone who thinks logically provides a nice contrast to the real world.

CROUCHING TIGER, HIDDEN DRAGON

A Chinese man had three daughters, he asked his eldest daughter what kind of man she would like to marry. "I would like to marry a man with three dragons on his chest", said the eldest daughter.

He then asked his second daughter who she would like to marry. "I would like to marry a man with two dragons on his chest," said the second daughter.

He finally asked his youngest daughter who she would like to marry. The youngest daughter replies, "I would like to marry a man with one draggin' on the ground."

WAR OF THE SEXES

A man and a woman who have never met before find themselves in the same sleeping carriage of a train. After the initial embarrassment, they both manage to get to sleep, the woman on the top bunk, the man on the lower. In the middle of the night, the woman leans over the side and says, "I'm sorry to bother you, but I'm awfully cold and I was wondering if you could possibly pass me another blanket."

The man leans out and, with a glint in his eye, says, "I've got a better idea... let's pretend we're married." "Why not?" giggles the woman. "Good", he replies. "Get your own bloody blanket."

A woman walks into the kitchen to find her husband stalking around with a fly swatter. "What are you doing?" she asks. "Hunting flies," he replies. "Oh! Killing any?" she asks. "Yep. Three males and two females," he replies. Intrigued, she asks, "How can you tell?" "Three were on a beer can and two were on the phone."

A blonde was driving down the motorway when her mobile phone rang. It was her husband, urgently warning her, "Honey, I just heard on the news that there's a car going the wrong way on the M25. Please be careful!" "It's not just one car," said the blonde. "There's hundreds of them!"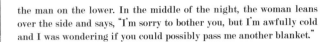

Q: Why do men break wind more than women? A: Because women can't shut up long enough to build up the required pressure.

Q: What's worse than a male chauvinist pig? A: A woman who won't do what she's told.

I haven't spoken to my wife for 18 months – I don't like to interrupt her.

Scientists have discovered a food that diminishes a woman's sex drive by 90 per cent. It's called a wedding cake.

Marriage is a three-ring circus: engagement ring, wedding ring and suffering.

Our last fight was my fault. My wife asked me, "What's on the TV?" I said, "Dust!"

In the beginning, God created the earth and rested. Then God created Man and rested. Then God created Woman. Since then, neither God nor Man has rested.

Young Son: "Dad, I heard that in some parts of Africa a man doesn't know his wife until he marries her. Is that true?" Dad: "That happens in every country, son."

A man inserted an advertisement in the classifieds: "Wife wanted." The next day he received a hundred letters. They all said the same thing: "You can have mine."

The most effective way to remember your wife's birthday is to forget it once.

Women will never be equal to men until they can walk down the street with a bald head and a beer gut and still think that they're beautiful.

THREE SISTERS

Three sisters, aged 92, 94 and 96, live in a house together. One night the 96-year-old draws a bath. She puts her foot in and pauses.

She hollers to the other sisters, "Was I gettin' in or out of the bath?" The 94-year-old yells back, "I don't know. I'll come up and see."

She starts up the stairs and pauses. "Was I going up the stairs or down?" she shouts.

The 92-year-old is sitting at the kitchen table having tea listening to her sisters. She shakes her head and says, "I sure hope I never get that forgetful." She knocks on wood for good measure and then yells, "I'll come up and help both of you as soon as I see who's at the door."

THEFT

An elderly Floridian calls 911 on her cell phone to report that her car has been broken into. She is hysterical as she explains her situation to the dispatcher, "They've stolen the stereo, the steering wheel, the brake pedal and even the accelerator!" she cries.

The dispatcher says, "Stay calm. An officer is on the way."

A few minutes later, the officer radios in. "Disregard," he says. "She got in the back seat by mistake."

NUTS

A preacher goes to a nursing home to meet an elderly parishioner. As he is sitting there he notices this bowl of peanuts beside her bed and takes one. As they talk, he can't help himself and eats one after another. By the time they are through talking, the bowl is empty. He says, "Ma'am, I'm so sorry, but I seem to have eaten all of your peanuts."

"That's OK," she says. "They would have just sat there. Without my teeth, all I can do with M&Ms is suck the chocolate off and put them back in the bowl."

DRIVEN MAD

A woman walks into a Lexus dealership. She browses around, then spots the perfect car and walks over to inspect it. As she bends to feel the fine leather upholstery, a loud fart escapes her. Very embarrassed, she looks around nervously to see if anyone has noticed her little accident and hopes a sales person doesn't pop up right now. But, as she turns back, standing next to her is a salesman. "Good day, madam. How may we help you today?" Very uncomfortably, she asks, "Sir, what is the price of this lovely vehicle?"

He answers, "Madam, I'm very sorry to say that if you farted just touching it, you're going to shit yourself when you hear the price."

$$ & & & & & & & & & & & & & & &

TRUTH HURTS

Sadly, Dave was born without ears and though he proved to be successful in business, his problem annoyed him greatly. One day he needed to hire a new manager for his company, so he set up three interviews. The first guy was great. He knew everything he needed to know and was very interesting, but at the end of the interview, Dave asked him, "Do you notice anything different about me?"

"Why, yes, I couldn't help but notice that you have no ears," came the reply.

Dave did not appreciate his honesty and threw him out of the office. The second interview was with a woman, and she was even better than the first guy. But he asked her the same question, "Do you notice anything different about me?"

"Well," she said, stammering, "you don't appear to have any ears." Dave again got upset and chucked her out in a rage. The third and final interviewee was the best of the bunch. He was a young man who had recently earned his MBA. He was smart, he was handsome, and he seemed to be a better businessman than the first two put together.

Dave was anxious, but went ahead and asked the young man the same question. "Do you notice anything different about me?"
Much to his surprise, the young man answered, "Yes, you wear contact lenses, don't you?"

Dave was shocked and realised this was an incredibly observant person. "How in the world did you know that?" he asked.
The young man fell off his chair laughing hysterically and replied, "Well, it's pretty hard to wear glasses with no bloody ears!"

MEN'S SECRET RULES

1. Any man who brings a camera to a stag night may be legally killed and eaten by his fellow partygoers.

2. Under no circumstances may two men share an umbrella.

3. It is OK for a man to cry under the following circumstances:
   a. When a heroic dog dies to save its master.
   b. The moment Angelina Jolie starts unbuttoning her blouse.
   c. After wrecking your boss's car.
   d. One hour, 12 minutes, 37 seconds into "The Crying Game" (but don't worry too much, it's an actress rather than an actor).
   e. When she is using her teeth.

4. Unless he murdered someone in your family, you must bail a friend out of jail within 12 hours.

5. If you've known a bloke for more than 24 hours, his sister is off limits forever, unless you actually marry her.

6. Moaning about the brand of free beer in a mate's fridge is forbidden. Complain at will if the temperature is unsuitable though.

7. No man shall ever be required to buy a birthday present for another man. In fact, even remembering your mate's birthday is strictly optional.

8. On a road trip, the strongest bladder determines pit stops, not the weakest.

9. When stumbling upon other blokes watching a sporting event, you may ask the score of the game in progress, but you may never ask who's playing.

10. You may fart in front of a woman only after you have brought her to climax. If you trap her head under the covers for the purpose of flatulent entertainment, she's officially your girlfriend.

11. It is permissible to quaff a fruity alcopop drink only when you're sunning on a tropical beach... and only if it's delivered by a topless supermodel. And it's free.

12. Only in situations of moral and/or physical peril are you allowed to kick another bloke in the nuts.

13. Unless you're in prison, never fight naked.

14. Friends don't let friends wear Speedos. Ever. Issue closed.

15. If a man's fly is down, that's his problem, you didn't see anything.

16. Women who claim they "love to watch sports" must be treated as spies until they demonstrate knowledge of the game and the ability to drink as much as the other sports watchers.

17. You must offer heartfelt and public condolences over the death of a girlfriend's cat, even if it was you who secretly set it on fire and threw it into a ceiling fan.

18. A man out and about with a hot, suggestively dressed woman must remain sober enough to fight.

19. Never hesitate to reach for the last beer or the last slice of pizza, but not both - that's just mean.

20. If you compliment a bloke on his six-pack, you'd better be talking about his choice of beer.

21. Never join your girlfriend or wife in making jokes at a mate of yours, unless she's withholding sex pending your response.

22. Phrases that may not be uttered to another man while lifting weights:
 a. Yeah, baby, push it!
 b. C'mon, give me one more! Harder!
 c. Another set and we can hit the showers!

23. Never talk to a man in a toilet unless you are on equal footing, i.e. both urinating, both waiting in line, etc. For all other situations, an almost imperceptible nod is all the conversation you need.

24. Never allow a conversation with a woman to go on longer than you are able to have sex with her. Keep a stopwatch by the phone. Hang up if necessary.

25. You cannot grass on a colleague who shows up at work with a massive hangover. You may however hide the aspirin, smear his chair with cheese, turn the brightness dial all the way down so he thinks his monitor is broken and have him paged over the loud speaker every seven minutes.

26. The morning after you and a girl who was formerly "just a friend" have wild, drunken badger sex, the fact that you're feeling weird and guilty is no reason not to nail her again before the discussion about what a big mistake it was.

27. It is acceptable for you to drive her car. It is not acceptable for her to drive yours.

28. Thou shalt not buy a car with an engine capacity of less than 1.5 litres.

29. Thou shalt not buy a car in the colours of brown, pink, lime green, orange or sky blue.

30. The woman who replies to the question "What do you want for Christmas?" with "If you loved me, you'd know what I want!" gets an Xbox 360.

IMPRESSIVE

For a man to impress a woman...
Wine her,
Dine her,
Call her,
Hug her,
Support her,
Hold her,
Compliment her,
Smile at her,
Listen to her,
Laugh with her,
Cry with her,
Romance her,
Encourage her,

Believe in her,
Pray with her,
Pray for her,
Cuddle with her,
Shop with her,
Give her jewellery,
Buy her flowers,
Hold her hand,
Write love letters to her,
And go to the end of the Earth and back again for her.

For a woman to impress a man...
Show up naked,
Bring food,
Don't block the TV.

GOD'S UBIQUITOUS QUALITY MANAGEMENT QUESTIONNAIRE

God would like to thank you for your belief, patronage and continued generous weekly donations. In order to better serve your needs, He asks that you take a few moments to answer the following questions. Please keep in mind that your responses will be kept completely confidential and that you need not disclose your name or address unless you prefer a direct response to comments or suggestions.

1. How did you find out about God?
- Bible
- Book of Mormon
- Torah
- Other book
- Visitation
- Dead Sea scrolls
- Near death experience

- Divine Inspiration
- Burning shrubbery
- Local Radio
- Request for information from Vatican
- Offer on back of cereal packet
- Evangelical television
- Trailer at local cinema
- Newspaper
- Arecibo radio telescope
- Internet site
- Word of mouth
- Other (please specify): _____

2. Which God did you acquire?
- Yahweh
- Jehovah
- Allah
- Krishna
- Buddha
- Ain Soph
- Father, Son & Holy Ghost (Trinity pack)
- Zeus and entourage (Olympus pack)
- Odin and entourage (Valhalla pack)
- Gaia/Goddess/Mother Nature (Pagan pack)
- Eris and assorted sages (Discordian Pack)
- Papa Legba and diverse Lwa (Voudon Pack)
- None of the above; I was taken in by a false god

3. Did your God come to you undamaged, with all parts in good working order and with no obvious breakage or missing attributes?
-Yes
-No
If no, please describe the problems you initially encountered here (please check all that apply)

- Not eternal
- Not omniscient
- Not omnipotent
- Makes mistakes
- Finite in space / does not occupy or inhabit the entire universe
- Permits sex outside of marriage
- Prohibits sex outside of marriage
- When beseeched, doesn't stay beseeched
- Plays dice with the universe
- Requires burnt offerings
- Requires virgin sacrifices
- Requires burnt virgins

4. Which factors were relevant in your decision to acquire a God?
(please check all that apply)
- Indoctrinated by parents
- Indoctrinated by society
- Needed reason to live
- Needed target for rage
- Imaginary friend grew up
- Hate to think for self
- Wanted to meet girls/boys
- Afraid of death
- Wanted to piss off parents
- Needed a day away from work
- Enjoy organ music
- Wanted to feel morally superior
- Graduated from the tooth fairy
- My shrubbery caught fire and told me to do it

5. Are you currently using any other source
of inspiration in addition to God? (please check all that apply)
- Television
- Money

- The Atkins Diet
- Football
- Cross-dressing/BDSM
- Kylie Minogue
- Burning shrubbery
- Ursula Andress
- Sex, drugs and rock & roll
- HAL 9000
- Dianetics
- Playboy and/or Playgirl
- Biorhythms
- Area 51
- Extra sensory perception
- Mantras
- Crystals (not including Crystal Gayle)
- Human sacrifices
- Wandering around in desert
- Other (please specify): _____

6. Are you currently worshipping a false god or have you ever previously done so? If so, which false God were you seduced by? (please check all that apply)
- George Bush
- Cthulhu
- The National Lottery
- Lucifer
- The Almighty Dollar
- The Conservative Right
- Mick Jagger
- Bill Gates
- Pug/Tomas
- Halloween Jack
- Orcus
- J.R. from Dallas

- Sauron
- Mushrooms
- Other (please specify): _____

7. God employs a limited degree of divine intervention, to preserve the balanced levels between miraculous presence and blind faith. Which would you prefer (circle one only):
a. More divine intervention
b. Less divine intervention
c. Current level of divine intervention is just right
d. Don't know – what's divine intervention?

8. God also attempts to maintain a balanced level of disasters and miracles. Please rate on a scale of 1 to 5 God's handling of the following (1 = unsatisfactory, 5 = excellent):

Flood	1	2	3	4	5
Pestilence	1	2	3	4	5
Earthquake	1	2	3	4	5
Death	1	2	3	4	5
War	1	2	3	4	5
Plague	1	2	3	4	5
Famine	1	2	3	4	5
AOL	1	2	3	4	5
David Beckham	1	2	3	4	5

Republican Congress	1	2	3	4	5
Dubya	1	2	3	4	5
My present relationship	1	2	3	4	5
My last relationship	1	2	3	4	5
Miracles Rescues	1	2	3	4	5
Spontaneous remissions	1	2	3	4	5
Crying statues	1	2	3	4	5
Water changing to wine	1	2	3	4	5
Walking on water	1	2	3	4	5
Stars hovering over towns	1	2	3	4	5
VCRs that set their own clocks	1	2	3	4	5
Clear and competent statements by the president	1	2	3	4	5
My present relationship	1	2	3	4	5
My last relationship	1	2	3	4	5

9. Please rate on a scale of 1 to 5 the following (1 = unsatisfactory, 5 = excellent)

God's courtesy	1	2	3	4	5

His answers to your prayers	1	2	3	4	5
How well your spiritual needs are being met	1	2	3	4	5
How well your shrubs are doing	1	2	3	4	5

10. Do you have any additional comments or suggestions for improving the quality of God's services? (attach additional sheet(s) if necessary)

TRUTH HURTS AGAIN

There was a middle-age couple that had two stunningly beautiful teenage daughters. The couple decided to try one last time for the son they always wanted. After months of trying, the wife became pregnant and, sure enough, delivered a healthy baby boy nine months later. The joyful father rushed to the nursery to see his new son. He took one look and was horrified to find the ugliest child he had ever seen.

He went to his wife and said that there was no way that he could be the father of the child. "Look at the two beautiful daughters I fathered," he cried. Then he gave her a stern look and asked, "Have you been fooling around on me?" The wife smiled sweetly and said, "Not this time."

BLESS YOU MA'AM

A man and a woman are sitting beside each other in the first class section of the plane. The woman sneezes, takes a tissue, gently wipes her nose and shudders quite violently in her seat. The man isn't sure why she is shuddering and goes back to reading. A few minutes pass. The woman sneezes again. She takes a tissue, gently wipes her nose and shudders quite violently in her seat. The man is becoming more and more curious about the shuddering. A few more minutes pass. The woman sneezes yet again. She takes a tissue, gently wipes her nose and shudders violently again.

The man has finally had all he can handle. He turns to the woman and says, "Three times you've sneezed and three times you've taken a tissue and wiped your nose then shuddered violently! Are you sending me signals, or are you going crazy?"
The woman replies, "I'm sorry if I disturbed you. I have a rare condition and when I sneeze, I have an orgasm."

The man, now feeling a little embarrassed but even more curious says, "I've never heard of that before. What are you taking for it?"
The woman looks at him and says, smiling dreamily, "Pepper."

STUNNING NUMBERS

3 Brits die each year testing if a 9v battery works on their tongue.

142 Brits were injured in 1999 by not removing all the pins from new shirts.

58 Brits are injured each year by using sharp knives instead of screwdrivers.

31 Brits have died since 1996 by watering their Christmas tree while the fairy lights were plugged in.

19 Brits have died in the last 3 years believing that Christmas decorations were chocolate.

British Hospitals reported 4 broken arms last year after cracker-pulling accidents.

101 people since 1999 have had broken parts of plastic toys pulled out of the soles of their feet.

18 Brits had serious burns in 2000 trying on a jumper with a lit cigarette in their mouth.

A massive 543 Brits were admitted to A&E in the last two years after opening bottles of beer with their teeth.

5 Brits were injured last year in accidents involving out of control Scalextric cars.
and finally... In 2000, 8 Brits cracked their skull whilst throwing up in the toilet.

GEORGE W. BUSH'S PRESIDENTIAL QUOTES! THIS IS FANTASTIC... AND TRUE!

"More and more of our imports are coming from outside the country."

"The inhabitants of Greece are the Greecians."

"The French don't have a word for 'entrepreneur.'"

"If we don't succeed, we run the risk of failure."

"I have made good judgments in the past. I have made good judgments in the future."

"The future will be better tomorrow."

"We're going to have the best educated American people in the world."

"I stand by all the misstatements that I've made."

"For NASA, space is still a high priority."

"We have a firm commitment to NATO, we are a part of NATO. We have a firm commitment to Europe. We are a part of Europe."

"A low voter turnout is an indication of fewer people going to the polls."

"Quite frankly, teachers are the only profession that teach our children."

"It isn't pollution that's harming the environment. It's the impurities in our air and water that are doing it."

"It's time for the human race to enter the solar system."

"General Musharraf of Pakistan is a Democrat."

THE MOST INTELLIGENT
PRESIDENT ON THE PLANET

An aircraft is about to crash. There are five passengers on board, but unfortunately only four parachutes.

The first passenger says, "I'm Shaquille O'Neill, the best NBA basketball player. The Lakers need me, it would be unfair to them if I died." So he takes the first parachute and jumps.

The second passenger, Hilary Clinton, says, "I am the wife of the former President of the United States. I am also a Senator in New York and America's potential future President. I am the guardian of morality, the voice of reason, and the most important woman ever. The world would be in deep trouble without me." She takes one of the parachutes and jumps.

The third passenger, George W. Bush, says, " I am the President of the United States of America. I have a huge responsibility in world politics. And apart from that, I am the most intelligent President in the history of the country and I have a responsibility to my people not to die". So he takes a parachute and jumps.

The fourth passenger, the Pope, says to the fifth passenger, a ten-year-old schoolboy, "I am already old. I have already lived my life, and I know where I am going when I die. My child, please, you take the last parachute."

The boy replies, "No problem Holy Father, there is still a parachute for each of us. America's most intelligent President just took my schoolbag."

SNIFFER

A man is sitting in an airliner which is about to takeoff, when a man with a Labrador Retriever occupies the empty seats alongside. The Lab is situated in the middle and the first man is looking quizzically at the dog when the second man explains that they work for the airline. The airline rep said, "Don't mind Sniffer. He is a sniffing dog, the best there is. I'll show you once we get airborne when I put him to work."

The plane takes off and levels out when the handler says to the first man, "Watch this." He tells the dog, "Sniffer, search."

Sniffer jumps down, walks along the aisle and sits next to a woman for a few seconds. It then returns to its seat and puts one paw on the handler's arm, who says, "Good boy." The airline rep turns to the first man and says, "That woman is in possession of marijuana, so I'm making a note of this and her seat number, so the police can apprehend her on arrival."

"Fantastic!" replies the first man.

Once again the rep sends Sniffer to search the aisles. The Lab sniffs about, sits down beside a man for a few seconds, returns to its seat and places two paws on the handler's arm. The airline rep says, "That man is carrying cocaine, so again I'm making a note of this and the seat number."
"I like it!" says the first man.

A third time the rep sends Sniffer to search the aisles. Sniffer goes up and down the plane and after a while sits down next to someone. He then comes racing back, jumps up onto his seat and craps all over the place. The first man is really grossed out by this behaviour from a supposedly well-trained sniffing dog and asks, "What's going on?"

The handler nervously replies, "He just found a bomb!"

REACHES THE PARTS
OTHER BEERS...

A man is waiting for his wife to give birth. The doctor comes in and informs him that his son was born without torso, arms or legs. The son is just a head! But the dad loves his son and raises him as well as he can, with love and compassion. After 18 years, the son is old enough for his first drink. Dad takes him to the bar, tearfully tells the son he is proud of him and orders up the biggest, strongest drink for his boy.

With all the bar patrons looking on curiously and the bartender shaking his head in disbelief, the boy takes his first sip of alcohol. Swoooop! A torso pops out! The bar is dead silent; then bursts into a whoop of joy.

The father, shocked, begs his son to drink again. The patrons chant "Take another drink!" The bartender still shakes his head in dismay. Swoooop! Two arms pops out. The bar goes wild. The father, crying and wailing, begs his son to drink again. The patrons chant "Take another drink!" The bartender ignores the whole affair.

By now the boy is getting tipsy and with his new hands he reaches down, grabs his drink and guzzles the last of it. Swoooop! Two legs pop out. The bar is in chaos. The father falls to his knees and tearfully thanks God.

The boy stands up on his new legs and stumbles to the left.... then to the right.... right through the front door, into the street, where a truck runs over him and kills him instantly. The bar falls silent. The father moans in grief. The bartender sighs and says: "He should have quit while he was a head!"

DOG DRIVING

As I drove into the parking lot, I noticed that a pickup truck with a dog sitting behind the wheel was rolling toward a female pedestrian. She seemed oblivious to the fact, so I hit my horn to get her attention. She looked up just in time to jump out of the way of the truck's path and the vehicle bumped harmlessly into the curb and stopped. I rushed to the woman's side to see if she was all right. "I'm fine," she assured me, "but I hate to think what could have happened to me if that dog hadn't honked."

MONKEYING AROUND

A police officer came upon a terrible wreck where the driver and the passenger had been killed. As he looked upon the wreckage, a little monkey came out of the brush and hopped around the crashed car. The officer looked down at the monkey and said: "I wish you could talk."

The monkey looked up at the officer and nodded his head up and down.

"You can understand what I'm saying?" said the officer.

Again, the monkey nodded his head up and down. "Well, did you see the accident?"

"Yes," nodded the monkey.

"What happened?"

The monkey pretended to have a can in his hand and turned it up by his mouth.

"They were drinking?" asked the officer.

"Yes," nodded the monkey.

"What else?" asked the officer.

The monkey pinched his fingers together and held them to his mouth, sucking inward quickly.

"They were smoking reefers too?" said the officer.

"Yes," nodded the monkey.

"What else?" queried the officer.

The monkey made a sexual gesture with his fingers.

"So they were playing around too?" asked the astounded officer.

"Yes," nodded the monkey.

"Now wait, you're saying your owners were drinking, smoking and playing around before they wrecked the car?"

"Yes," the monkey nodded.

"What were you doing during all this?" asked the officer.

The monkey reaches out to grab an imaginary steering wheel.

STRANGE, IT ALSO WORKED FOR YOUR NOSE...

Fresh from her shower, a woman stands in front of the mirror, complaining to her husband that her breasts are too small. Instead of his standard response of reassuring her that that isn't the case, her husband uncharacteristically comes up with a suggestion. "If you want your breasts to grow, then take a piece of toilet paper and rub it between your breasts for a few seconds every day."

Willing to try anything, the wife fetches a piece of toilet paper and stands in front of the mirror, rubbing it between her breasts. "How long will this take?" she asks.

"They'll grow larger over a period of years," he replies.

The wife stops. "Why do you think rubbing a piece of toilet paper between my breasts every day will make my breasts grow over the years?"

He shrugged and said, "Worked for your arse, didn't it?"

HI-TECH CRAP!

Three men, one American, one Japanese and one Irish, were sitting naked in the sauna. Suddenly there was a beeping sound. The American pressed his forearm and the beep stopped. The others looked at him questioningly. "That was my pager," he said. "I have a microchip under the skin of my arm."

A few minutes later a phone rang. The Japanese fellow lifted his palm to his ear and had a short conversation. When he finished he explained, "That was my mobile phone. I have a microchip in my hand."

Paddy felt decidedly low-tech. So as not to be outdone, he decided he had to do something just as impressive. He stepped out of the sauna and went to the toilet. He returned with a piece of toilet paper hanging from his arse. The others raised their eyebrows. "Will you look at that," said Paddy. "I'm getting a fax."

SIXTH-DEGREE VD

There was this little boy about 12 years old walking down the sidewalk, dragging a flattened frog on a string behind him. He came up to the doorstep of a house of ill repute and knocked on the door. When the madam answered it, she saw the little boy and asked what he wanted. He said, "I want to have sex with one of the women inside. I have the money to buy it, and I'm not leaving until I get it." The madam figured, why not, so she told him to come in. Once in, she told him to pick any of the girls he liked. He asked, "Do any of the girls have any diseases?" Of course the madam said no. He said, "I heard all the men talking about having to get shots after having sex with Amber. THAT'S the girl I want."

Since the little boy was so adamant and had the money to pay for it, the madam told him to go to the first room on the right. He headed down the hall dragging the squashed frog behind him. Ten minutes later he came back, still dragging the frog, paid the madam and headed out the door. The madam stopped him and asked, "Why did you pick the only girl in the place with a disease, instead of one of the others?"

He said, "Well, if you must know, tonight my parents are going out to a restaurant to eat, leaving me at home with the baby-sitter. After they leave, my baby-sitter will have sex with me, because she's got a nasty fetish for cute little boys. She will then get the disease that I just caught. When Mum and Dad get back, Dad will take the baby-sitter home. On the way, he'll screw the baby-sitter, and he'll catch the disease. Then when Dad gets home from the baby-sitter's, he and Mum will go to bed and have sex and Mum will catch it. In the morning when Dad goes to work, the milkman will deliver the milk, have a quickie with Mum and catch the disease, and HE'S the son-of-a-bitch who ran over my FROG!"

IF YOU CAN READ THIS, THE BIRD FELL OFF THE BIKE...

An Irishman who had a little too much to drink is driving home from the city one night and, of course, his car is weaving violently all over the road. A cop pulls him over. "So," says the cop to the driver, "where have ya been?"

"Why, I've been to the pub of course," slurs the drunk.

"Well," says the cop, "it looks like you've had quite a few to drink this evening."

"I did all right," the drunk says with a smile.

"Did you know," says the cop, standing straight and folding his arms across his chest, "that a few junctions back, your wife fell out of your car?"

"Oh, thank heavens," sighs the drunk. "For a minute there, I thought I'd gone deaf."

THE TIGER PUZZLE....

Alex Ferguson calls Beckham into his office. "David," he says, "I need to talk to you about your performance against Leeds the other night.

You were bloody hopeless, completely off form."

"Sorry boss", says David. "I've not been meself lately. I got problems at home, right."

"Oh dear", says Fergie. "What's up? Posh and the kids ok?"

"Oh, they're fine right, it's just that something is really bugging me right, and I'm losing sleep and everything, right? I can't concentrate on me football and it's really messing me head up."

"Whatever's the matter?" says Fergie,

"Well boss, It's pretty serious. Victoria bought this jigsaw puzzle the other day right and..."

"A JIGSAW??" shouts Sir Alex. "You're playing like that because of a bloody jigsaw?"

"Yeah boss, but you don't understand right, it's really doing me head in!" says David, "It's really hard, it's this picture of a Tiger and it looks really easy on the box right and I'm sure I've got all the bits and everything but I just can't get it to work and it's doing me head in and and..."

"David, David, David" says Fergie,
"You'd better get a grip son, and quick."

"Ok boss, but... It's this picture of a Tiger right and it looks really easy on the box, right and I'm sure I got all the bits right and everything but can't do it and it's doing my head in and....and...it's a Tiger, right and it looks easy but it's really hard, right and er, it's a Tiger and everything, er...on the box...er...sorry boss."

"Ok, Ok" says Sir Alex, "bring the jigsaw in and let's have a look shall we. It can't be that difficult."

"Thanks boss," says David. So Becks brings in the jigsaw and takes it to Fergie's office.

"Here it is boss", he says, showing Ferguson the picture on the box. "Look boss, it's a Tiger, right and it's a really good picture and everything but I just can't do it and it's really hard and its doing my head in and everything innit." Becks empties all the pieces from the box all over Fergie's desk.

Sir Alex looks at what's on the desk, looks up with his head in his hands and says to Beckham. "Put the Frosties back in the box, David..."

WHAT DID YOU DO IN THE GREAT WAR?

An elderly Italian man asked a local priest to hear his confession. "Father, during the Second World War a beautiful woman knocked on my door and asked me to hide her from the Nazis. I hid her in my attic."

The priest replied, "That was a wonderful thing you did."

"It's worse than just that though, Father. I told her she must repay me with sexual favours."

"You were both in great danger and would have suffered terribly if you were caught, God will balance the good and the evil and judge you kindly. You are forgiven."

"Thank you father. That's a great load off my mind. I have one more question."

"Yes?" prompted the priest.

"Should I tell her the war is over?"

LEGAL AND GENERAL

Two physicians boarded a flight out of Seattle. One sat in the window seat, the other sat in the middle seat. Just before takeoff, an attorney got on and took the aisle seat next to the two physicians. The attorney kicked off his shoes, wiggled his toes and was settling in when the physician in the window seat said, "I think I'll get up and get a coke."

>> 100

"No problem," said the attorney, "I'll get it for you." While he was gone, one of the physicians picked up the attorney's shoe and spat in it.

When he returned with the coke, the other physician said, "That looks good, I think I'll have one, too."

Again, the attorney obligingly went to fetch it and while he was gone, the other physician picked up the other shoe and spat in it. The attorney returned and they all sat back and enjoyed the flight. As the plane was landing, the attorney slipped his feet into his shoes and knew immediately what had happened.

"How long must this go on?" he asked. "This fighting between our professions? This hatred? This animosity? This spitting in shoes and pissing in cokes?"

CORPORATE LESSON 3

Case: A sales rep, an administration clerk and their manager are walking to lunch when they find an antique oil lamp. They rub it and a genie comes out in a puff of smoke. The genie considers the situation and says, "I usually only grant three wishes, so I'll give each of you just one."

"Me first! Me first!" says the admin clerk. "I want to be in the Bahamas, driving a speedboat, without a care in the world." Poof! She's gone.

In astonishment, "Me next! Me next!" says the sales rep. "I want to be in Hawaii, relaxing on the beach with my personal masseuse, an endless supply of pina coladas, and the love of my life."

Poof! He's gone. "OK, you're up," the genie says to the manager.

The manager says, "I want those two back in the office after lunch."

Analysis: Always let your boss have the first say.

HONEYMOONERS

A posh hotel holds three weddings on the same day and at the end of the night, the three grooms meet up at the bar to discuss the day's events over a couple of beers. One questions the other two, "Listen, it's our wedding night and I was wondering... er... how many times are we expected to... um... you know... DO IT?"

They discuss this for a while. Eventually, they all decide to retire to their respective wives and see how the night goes, with the idea to meet up the following morning over breakfast to discuss what went on. Suddenly one of the grooms pipes up, "Hold on lads, we can't discuss our first night marital goings-on over the breakfast table with our new wives sitting there with us."

"No you're right," says another, "What we'll do then, is for every piece of toast we order with our breakfast, that'll be the amount of times we did it."

They all decide it's an excellent idea and depart. The next day in the hotel dining room, the grooms are all looking a bit dishevelled, but that's nothing compared to the brides, who can barely stagger across the room to their tables.

The waitress comes up to the first groom to take his order. "Good morning young lady, I would like to have the full English breakfast with THREE pieces of fine buttered toast please." He says proudly.

The other two grooms smile at him and raise a glass of fresh orange in a toast to his fantastic prowess. The waitress moves to the second couple and the groom orders, "I

too shall have the full English breakfast but could I have FOUR pieces of toast."

The waitress gets to the last groom. "I shall also have the full English breakfast please, but I shall have..." He takes a deep breath. "SEVEN PIECES OF TOAST," he says. He gives a big cheesy grin to his two wedding mates, who stare in disbelief. "Seven pieces of toast, sir?" queries the waitress. "Why, that's an awful lot." "Yes indeed, young lady, seven pieces of toast."

She writes down his order and turns away, but before she can leave, the groom calls after her again. "By the way my dear, can you make three of those brown?"

SNAPPIES

Q: What do you call a Frenchman wearing sandals?
A: Philippe Phlop.

Q: What's the difference between a tea bag and Tottenham Hotspur?
A: A tea bag stays in the cup longer.

An Al-Qaeda terrorist has been found dead in a homosexual's swimming pool. Police suspect it was a suicide bumming.

NEW PHRASES

AEROPLANE BLONDE: One who has bleached/dyed her hair but still has a 'black box'.

AUSSIE KISS: Similar to a French Kiss, but given down under.

BADLY PACKED KEBAB: A vulgar (but still excellent) term for the female genitalia.

BEER COAT: The invisible but warm coat worn when walking home after a pub crawl at 3 in the morning.

BEER COMPASS: The invisible device that ensures your safe arrival home after a pub crawl, even though you're too pissed to remember where you live, how to get there, or where you've come from.

BEER SCOOTER: The ability to get home after a night out on the booze and not remember it, i.e. "I don't even remember getting home last night, I must have caught the beer scooter."

BOBFOC: Body Off Baywatch, Face Off Crimewatch.

BOOZEPOINT: A modern term for a cash machine (ATM). Named so because it is common to visit one before going out on the booze.

BREAKING THE SEAL: Your first piss in the pub, usually after two hours of drinking. After breaking the seal of your bladder, repeat visits to the toilet will be required every 10 or 15 minutes for the rest of the night.

BRITNEY SPEARS: Modern Slang for 'beers', e.g. "Couple of Britneys please, Doreen".

BUDGIE'S TONGUE: An erect clitoris.

DOUBLE-BASS: A sexual position in which the man enters the woman from behind and then fiddles with the woman's nipples with one hand and her Budgie's Tongue with the other. The position is similar to that used when playing a double bass instrument, though the sound produced is slightly different.

ETCH-A-SKETCH: Trying to draw a smile on a woman's face by twiddling both of her nipples simultaneously.

FLOGGING ON: Surfing the Internet for some left-handed websites.

F**KS**tF**KS**tF**KS**t : The sound made when driving through too narrow a gap at too high a speed.

GLAND-TO-HAND COMBAT: A vigorous masturbation session.

GOING FOR A MCSHIT: Entering a fast food restaurant with no intention of buying food, just going to the bog. If challenged by a pimply staff member, your declaration to them that you'll buy their food afterwards is a 'McShit With Lies'.

GREYHOUND: A very short skirt, only an inch from the hare.

JOHNNY-NO-STARS: A young man of substandard intelligence, the typical adolescent who works in a burger restaurant. The stars come from the badges displaying stars that staff at fast-food restaurants often wear to show their level of training.

MILLENNIUM DOMES: The contents of a Wonderbra, i.e. extremely impressive when viewed from the outside, but there's actually fuck-all in there worth seeing.

MONKEY BATH: A bath so hot that when lowering yourself in, you go, "Oo! Oo! Aa! Aa! Aa!"

MUMBLER: An attractive girl in tight shorts or jeans, so that you can see the lips moving, but can't quite make out what they're saying.

MYSTERY BUS : The bus that arrives at the pub on Friday night, while you're in the toilet after your 10th pint, and whisks away all the unattractive people so the pub is suddenly packed with stunners when you come back in.

MYSTERY TAXI: The taxi that arrives at your place on Saturday morning before you wake up, whisks away the stunner you slept with, and leaves a ten-Pinter in your bed instead.

NELSON MANDELA: Rhyming Slang for Stella (Stella Artois, the lager).

PICASSO-ARSE : A woman whose knickers are too small for her, so she looks like she's got four buttocks.

SALAD DODGER: An American, from the national weight problem.

STARFISH TROOPER or ARSETRONAUT: A gay guy.

SWAMP-DONKEY: A deeply unattractive woman.

TART FUEL or BITCH PISS: Bottled Alcopops, e.g. Bacardi Breezers, regularly consumed by young women.

TITANIC: A lady who goes down first time out.

TODGER DODGER: A lesbian.

UP ON BLOCKS: Menstruating, from being out of action, as in a car in a garage, i.e. "I don't think I'll be in luck tonight lads, the missus is up on blocks."

WALLACE AND GROMIT: Rhyming Slang for 'vomit'.

WANK SEANCE: During a masturbation session, the eerie feeling that you're being watched with disgust by generations of dead relatives.

WYNONA RYDER: Rhyming Slang for 'cider', e.g. "Pint of Wynona, half a Nelson and a bottle of tart fuel for the mumbler there please, Doreen."

PLACE SWAPPING

A man was sick and tired of going to work every day while his wife stayed home. He wanted her to see what he went through so he prayed, "Dear Lord, I go to work every day and put in 8 hours while my wife merely stays at home. I want her to know what I go through, so please allow her body to switch with mine for a day. Amen."

God, in his infinite wisdom, granted the man's wish. The next morning, sure enough, the man awoke as a woman. He arose, cooked breakfast for his mate, woke up the kids, set out their school clothes, fed them breakfast, packed their lunches, drove them to school, came home and picked up the dry cleaning, took it to the cleaners and stopped at the bank to make a deposit, went grocery shopping, then drove home to put away the groceries, paid the bills and balanced the check book. He cleaned the cat's litter box and bathed the dog.

Then it was already one o'clock and he hurried to make the beds, do the laundry, vacuum, dust and sweep and mop the kitchen floor. He ran to the school to pick up the kids and got into an argument with them on the way home. He set out milk and cookies and got the kids organised to do their homework, then set up the ironing board and watched TV while he did the ironing. At 4:30 he began peeling potatoes and washing vegetables for salad, breaded the pork chops and snapped fresh beans for supper. After supper, he cleaned the kitchen, ran the dishwasher, folded laundry, bathed the kids and put them to bed. By 9pm he was exhausted and, though his daily chores weren't finished, he went to bed where he was expected to make love, which he managed to get through without complaint.

The next morning, he awoke and immediately knelt by the bed and said, "Lord, I don't know what I was thinking. I was so wrong to envy my wife staying at home all day. Please, oh please, let us trade back." The Lord, in his infinite wisdom, replied, "My son, I feel you have learned your lesson and I will be happy to change things back to the way they were. You'll have to wait nine months, though. You got pregnant last night."

JUST FOR YOU, JOHNNY BOY LOL!

Australian Etiquette Handbook

General rules:
1. Never take a beer to a job interview.
2. Don't burn rubber while travelling in a funeral procession.
3. It's tacky to take an esky to church.
4. Even if you're certain you're included in the will, it's rude to take a trailer to the funeral home.

Dining:
1. When decanting wine from the box, tilt the paper cup and pour slowly so as not to "bruise" the wine.
2. The centrepiece for a table should never be anything prepared by a taxidermist.

Personal hygiene:
1. While ears need to be cleaned regularly, this should be done in private, using one's OWN car keys.
2. Dirt and grease under the fingernails is a no-no, as they detract from a woman's jewellery and alter the taste of finger foods.

Dating (outside the family):
1. Always offer to bait your date's hook, especially on the first date.
2. Establish with her parents what time she's expected back. Some will say "10pm", others might say "Monday." If the latter is the answer, it's the man's responsibility to get her to school on time.

Theatre etiquette:
1. Crying babies should be taken to the lobby and picked up after the movie has ended.
2. Refrain from talking to characters on the screen. Tests have proven they can't hear you.

Weddings:
1. Livestock is a poor choice for a wedding gift.
2. For the groom, at least, rent a tux. A tracksuit with a cummerbund and a clean football jumper can create a tacky appearance.
3. Though uncomfortable, say "yes" to socks and shoes for the occasion.

Driving:
1. Dim your headlights for approaching vehicles, even if the gun's loaded and the kangaroo is in sight.
2. Never tow another car using panty hose and duct tape.
3. When sending your wife down the road with a petrol can, it's impolite to ask her to bring back beer, too.

I WANT ONE LIKE THAT... JET FIGHTER WARRANTY CARD

McDONNELL DOUGLAS CORPORATION: WARRANTY CARD

Thank you for purchasing a McDonnell Douglas military aircraft. In order to protect your new investment, please take a few moments to fill out the warranty registration card below. Answering the survey questions is not required, but the information will help us to develop new products that best meet your needs.

Title: _ Mr. _ Mrs. _ Ms. _ Miss _ Lt. _ Gen. _ Comrade _ Classified _ Other

First Name: .... **Initial:** .... **Last Name:** ....

Password: .... (max. 8 char)
Code Name: ....

Latitude-Longitude-Altitude: .... / .... / ....

Which model of aircraft did you purchase?
_ F-14 Tomcat _ F-15 Eagle _ F-16 Falcon _ F-117A Stealth
_ Classified

Date of purchase (Year/Month/Day): ..../..../....
Serial Number: ....

Please indicate where this product was purchased:
_ Received as gift/aid package _ Catalogue/showroom
_ Independent arms broker   _ Mail order
_ Discount store   _ Government surplus
_ Classified

Please indicate how you became aware of the McDonnell Douglas product you have just purchased:
_ Heard loud noise, looked up _ Store display
_ Espionage   _ Recommended by friend/relative/ally
_ Political lobbying by manufacturer   _ Was attacked by one

Please indicate the three factors that most influenced your decision to purchase this McDonnell Douglas product:
_ Style/appearance
_ Speed/manoeuvrability
_ Price/value
_ Comfort/convenience
_ Kickback/bribe
_ Recommended by salesperson
_ McDonnell Douglas' reputation
_ Advanced Weapons Systems
_ Backroom politics
_ Negative experience opposing one in combat

Please indicate the location(s) where this product will be used:
_ North America   _ Iraq   _ Aircraft carrier
_ Iraq   _ Europe _ Iraq
_ Middle East (not Iraq)   _ Iraq   _ Africa
_ Iraq   _ Asia/Far East   _ Iraq
_ Misc Third World countries _ Classified
_ Oh all right then, Iraq Please indicate the
products that you cur

Rently own or intend to purchase in the near future:
_ Colour TV   _ VCR   _ ICBM
_ Killer Satellite   _ DVD Player   _ Air-to-Air Missiles
_ Space Shuttle (out of stock) _ Home Computer _   Nuclear
Weapon (clean/dirty)

How would you describe yourself or your organisation?

(indicate all that apply)
_ **Communist**
_ **Capitalist/Monetarist**
_ **Socialist**
_ **Terrorist**
_ **Crazed**
_ **Neutral**
_ **Democratic**
_ **Dictatorship**
_ **Corrupt**
_ **Primitive/Tribal**
_ **American puppet regime**

How did you pay for your McDonnell Douglas product?
_ **Deficit spending**
_ **Cash**
_ **Suitcases of cocaine**
_ **Iraq oil revenues**
_ **Personal cheque**
_ **Credit card**
_ **Ransom money**
_ **Traveller's cheque**
_ **Transfer from Swiss account**

12. Your occupation:
_ **Homemaker**   _ **Sales / Marketing** _ **Revolutionary**
_ **Clerical** _ **Mercenary**   _ **Tyrant**
_ **Middle management**   _ **Eccentric billionaire**
_ **Defence Minister / General**
_ **Retired** _ **Student** _ **Unemployed**

To help us better understand our customers, please indicate the
interests and activities in which you and your spouse enjoy par-
ticipating on a regular basis:
_ **Golf**   _ **Boating / Sailing** _ **Sabotage**
_ **Running / Jogging** _ **Propaganda / Misinformation**
_ **Destabilisation / Overthrow**
_ **Defaulting on loans**   _ **Gardening**   _ **Crafts**
_ **Black Market / Smuggling** _ **Collectibles**
_ **Watching sports on TV**
_ **Wines** _ **Interrogation / Torture**   _ **Household pets**
_ **Crushing rebellions**   _ **Espionage**
_ **Fashion & Clothing**
_ **Border disputes**   _ **Mutually Assured Destruction** _ **Religious
homicidal frenzy**

Thank you for taking the time to fill out this questionnaire. Your
answers will be used in market studies that will help McDonnell

Douglas serve you better in the future as well as allowing you to receive mailings and special offers from other companies, governments, extremist groups, and mysterious consortia. As a bonus for responding to this survey, you will be registered for the chance to win a brand new F-117A in our Desert Thunder Sweepstakes!

If you have comments or suggestions about our fighter planes, please write to: **McDONNELL DOUGLAS CORPORATION**, Marketing Department, Military, Aerospace Division
****

IMPORTANT: This email is intended for the use of the individual addressee(s) named above and may contain information that is confidential, privileged or unsuitable for overly sensitive persons with low self-esteem, no sense of humour or irrational religious beliefs. If you are not the intended recipient, any dissemination, distribution or copying of this email is not authorised (either explicitly or implicitly) and constitutes an irritating social faux pas. Unless the word absquatulation has been used in its correct context somewhere other than in this warning, it does not have any legal or grammatical use and may be ignored. No animals were harmed in the transmission of this email, although the kelpie next door is living on borrowed time, let me tell you. Those of you with an overwhelming fear of the unknown will be gratified to learn that there is no hidden message revealed by reading this warning backwards, so just ignore that Alert Notice from Microsoft. However, by pouring a complete circle of salt around yourself and your computer you can ensure that no harm befalls you and your pets. If you have received this email in error, please add some nutmeg and egg whites and place it in a warm oven for 40 minutes. Whisk briefly and let it stand for two hours before icing.

VIVA LAS VEGAS

A man comes home from work one day to find his wife sitting outside with her bags packed, He asks her what she is doing and she replies, "I'm going to Las Vegas." The man asks why she's decided to leave and she says, "I found out that I can make a lot of money doing what I give you for free. In Vegas you get paid $400 for giving someone oral sex."

The man ponders his wife's reply, goes into the house, packs his own bags and joins her outside. "And where do you think you're going?" She asks.

"I'm going to Las Vegas as well."

"Why?"

"I want to see how you're going to live on $400 a year."

EMPLOYEE OF THE MONTH...

These individual quotes were reportedly taken from actual employee performance evaluations. You may want to consider using them for someone you work with...

- Since my last report, this employee has reached rock bottom and has started to dig.
- His men would follow him anywhere, but only out of morbid curiosity.
- I would not allow this employee to breed.
- This employee is really not so much a has-been as a definitely won't be.
- Works well when under constant supervision and cornered like a rat in a trap.
- When she opens her mouth, it seems that it is only to change feet.
- He would be out of his depth in a car-park puddle.
- This young lady has delusions of adequacy.
- He sets low personal standards and then consistently fails to achieve them.
- This employee is depriving a village somewhere of an idiot.
- This employee should go far, and the sooner he starts, the better.
- Has a full six-pack, but lacks the plastic thing to hold it all together.
- A gross ignoramus –144 times worse than an ordinary ignoramus.
- He doesn't have ulcers, but he's a carrier.
- I would like to go hunting with him sometime.
- He's been working with glue too much.

- He would argue with a signpost.
- She brings a lot of joy whenever she leaves the room.
- If his IQ ever reaches 50, he should sell.
- If you see two people talking and one looks bored, he's the other one.
- A photographic memory with the lens cover glued on.
- A prime candidate for natural deselection.
- Donated her brain to science before she was done using it.
- Gates are down, the lights are flashing, but the train isn't coming.
- Has two brains – one is lost and the other is out looking for it.
- If he were any more stupid, he'd have to be watered twice a week.
- If you give him a penny for his thoughts, you'd get change.
- If you stand close enough to him, you can hear the oceans.
- It's hard to believe that he beat out 1,000,000 other sperm.
- One neuron short of a synapse.
- Some drink from the fountain of knowledge; she only gargled.
- The wheel is turning, but the hamster is dead.

AND YOU THINK YOU JUST HAD A BAD DAY AT THE OFFICE?

Rob is a commercial saturation diver for Global Divers in Louisiana. He performs underwater repairs on offshore drilling rigs. Below is an email he sent to his sister:

Hi Sue,
Just another note from your bottom-dwelling brother. Last week I had a bad day at the office. I know you've been feeling down lately at work, so I thought I would share my dilemma with you to make you realise it's not so bad after all. Before I can tell you what happened to me, I first must bore you with a few technicalities of my job.

As you know, my office lies at the bottom of the sea. I wear a suit to the office. It's a wetsuit. This time of year the water is quite cool. So what we do to keep warm is this: We have a diesel powered industrial water heater. This $20,000 piece of s**t sucks the water out of the sea. It heats it to a delightful temperature. It then pumps it down to the diver through a garden hose, which is taped to the air hose.

Now this sounds like a damn good plan, and I've used it several times with no complaints. What I do, when I get to the bottom and start working, is I take the hose and stuff it down the back of my wetsuit. This floods my whole suit with warm water. It's like working in a jacuzzi.

Everything was going well today until all of a sudden, my bum started to itch. So, of course, I scratched it. This only made things worse. Within a few seconds my arse started to burn. I pulled the hose out from my back, but the damage was done. In agony I realised what had happened. The hot water machine had sucked up a jellyfish and pumped it into my suit.

Now since I don't have any hair on my back, the jellyfish couldn't stick to it. However, the crack of my bum was not as fortunate. When I scratched what I thought was an itch, I was actually grinding the jellyfish into my ass.

I informed the dive supervisor of my dilemma over the communicator. His instructions were unclear due to the fact that he and with five other divers were all laughing hysterically.

Needless to say I aborted the dive. I was instructed to make three agonising in-water decompression stops totalling 35 minutes before I could reach the surface to begin my dry-chamber decompression. When I arrived at the surface, I was wearing nothing but my brass helmet. As I climbed out of the water, the medic, with tears of laughter running down his face, handed me a tube of cream and told me to rub it on my bum as soon as I got in the chamber. The cream put the fire out, but I couldn't s**t for two days because my arsehole was swollen shut.

LOVE YOU TO DEATH

Jake was dying. His wife, Becky, was maintaining a candlelight vigil by his side. She held his fragile hand, tears running down her face. Her praying roused him from his slumber. He looked up and his pale lips began to move slightly, "My darling Becky," he whispered.

"Hush, my love," she said. "Rest. Shhh, don't talk."

He was insistent. "Becky," he said in his tired voice, "I have something I must confess to you."

"There's nothing to confess," replied the weeping Becky. "Everything's all right. Go to sleep."

"No, no, I must die in peace, Becky. I'm so sorry. I slept with your sister and your best friend. I slept with her best friend. I even slept with your mother!"

"I know," Becky whispered softly. "That's why I poisoned you."

PUB CRAWL FOR FREE..
ER... NEARLY FREE...

John and Neil fancied a pint or two but didn't have a lot of money. Between them, they had a staggering 50 pence. Neil said, "Hang on. I've an idea." Off he went into the butchers shop next door and came out with one large Cumberland Sausage.

"Are you crazy?" John exclaimed. "Now we haven't got any money left at all."

"Don't worry, just follow me," said Simon and went into the pub where he ordered two pints and two large Jack Daniels.

"Now you have lost it. Do you know how much trouble we will be in? We haven't got any money!"

"Don't worry, I've got a plan. Cheers."

They had their drinks and Neil said, "OK, I will now stick the sausage through my zip – you get on your knees and put it in your mouth."

Said and done. The landlord noticed it, went berserk and threw them out. They continued this, pub after pub, getting more and more drunk – all for free. At the tenth pub John said, "Mate, I don't think I can continue this any longer. I am totally wasted and my knees are killing me."

"How do you think I feel?" Neil replied. "I lost the sausage in the third pub."

MAN, THIS ONE IS SOOOOOOOO SILLY... I HESITATE TO SEND IT TO YOU...

Far away in the tropical waters of the Caribbean, two prawns were swimming around in the sea – one called Justin and the other called Christian. The prawns were constantly being harassed and threatened by sharks that patrolled the area. Finally one day Justin said to Christian, "I'm bored and frustrated at being a prawn, I wish I was a shark, then I wouldn't have any worries about being eaten..."

As Justin had his mind firmly on becoming a predator, a mysterious cod appeared and said, "Your wish is granted." Lo and behold, Justin turned into a shark. Horrified, Christian immediately swam away, afraid of being eaten by his old mate.

Time went on and Justin found himself becoming bored and lonely as a shark. All his old mates simply swam away whenever he came close to them. Justin didn't realise that his new menacing appearance was the cause of his sad plight. While out swimming alone one day, he saw the mysterious cod again and couldn't believe his luck. Justin figured that the fish could change him back into a prawn. He begged the cod to change him back and, lo and behold, he was turned back into a prawn.

With tears of joy in his tiny little eyes, Justin swam back to his friends and bought them all a cocktail. Looking around the gathering at the reef, he searched for his old pal. "Where's Christian?" he asked.

"He's at home, distraught that his best friend joined the enemy and became a shark," came the reply.

Eager to put things right again, he set off to Christian's house. As he opened the coral gate the memories came flooding back. He banged on the door and shouted, "It's me, Justin, your old friend, come out and see me again."

Christian replied, "No way man, you'll eat me. You're a shark, the enemy, and I won't be tricked."

Justin cried back, "No, no I'm not. That was the old me. I've changed. I've seen Cod. I'm a prawn again, Christian."

VEGAS REVENGE...

A successful businessman flew to Vegas for the weekend to gamble. He even lost the shirt off his back, and had nothing left but a quarter and the second half of his round trip ticket. He desperately needed get to the airport so he could get himself home. So he went out to the front of the casino where there was a cab waiting. He got in and explained his situation to the cabby. He promised to send the driver money from home, he offered him his credit card numbers, his driver's license number, his address, etc. but all to no avail. The cabby just said, "If you don't have 15 dollars, get the hell out of my cab!"

The businessman was forced to hitchhike to the airport and was barely in time to catch his flight. One year later, the businessman, having worked long and hard to regain his financial success, returned to Vegas and this time, he won big. Feeling pretty good about himself, he went out to the front of the casino to get a cab ride back to the airport.

Well, who should he see out there, at the end of a long line of cabs, but the guy who had refused to give him a ride when he was down on his luck.

The businessman thought for a moment about how he could make the guy pay for his lack of charity, and he hit on a plan. He got in the first cab in the line, and said "How much for a ride to the airport?"

"15 dollars," came the reply.

"And how much for you to give me a blow job on the way?"

"What?! Get the hell of my cab, you pervert!"

The businessman got into the back of each cab in the long line and asked the same questions, with the same result, getting kicked out of each cab. When he got to his old nemesis at the back of the line, he got in and asked, "How much for a ride to the airport?" The cabby told him the same price as everyone else, and the businessman said "Ok." Off they went. As they drove slowly past the long line of cabs, the businessman gave a big smile and thumbs-up sign to each driver.

ASKING FOR TROUBLE

A tongue-tied man goes into a nut shop and the first thing he notices is that the guy behind the counter has the largest nose he's ever seen. The tongue-tied guy quickly turns his attention to the merchandise and asks, "Ess-tues me, sir?"

"Yes?" replies the clerk.

"Tould you tale me how mutsh your pisstasheos arr?"

"Pistachios? They're six dollars a pound."

"SSit!" The tongue-tied guy goes back to browsing and then asks, "Welp, how mutsh arr your aahhmons?"

"Almonds? They're seven fifty a pound."

"SSIT! tas pensive," replies the tongue-tied man. "Welp, how bout your pikanns?"

"Pecans? They're on sale today, they're only four fifty a pound."

"Welp, Ssit. Just div me a pound of dose dhen."

"All right then," says the clerk as he begins bagging up a pound of pecans.

Then the tongue-tied guy says to the clerk, "Sirr, I just wanna tay tank you fo not making fun of de way I talk, cauz I tan't hep it."

The clerk replies with a smile. "Oh sir, you don't have to thank me for that. I don't make fun of anybody. I don't know if you noticed but I have a rather large nose."

The tongue-tied guy replies, "Oh, is dat your noze? Given how high yourr fucken nuts arr, I figgerd it was your fucken cock."

GET YOUR PRIORITIES RIGHT

Mark returned from a doctor's visit one day and told his wife Alma that the doctor said he only had 24 hours to live. Wiping away her tears, he asked her to make love with him. Of course she agreed and they made passionate love. Six hours later, Mark went to her again and said, "Honey, now I only have 18 hours left to live. Maybe we could make love again?" Alma agrees and again they make love.

Later, Mark is getting into bed when he realised he now had only eight hours of life left. He touched Alma's shoulder and said, "Honey? Please? Just one more time before I die." She agreed, then rolled over and fell asleep. Mark, however, heard the clock ticking in his head and he tossed and turned until he was down to only four more hours. He tapped his wife on the shoulder to wake her up. "Honey, I only have four hours left! Could we...?" His wife sat up abruptly, turned to him and said, "God, Mark, you're so selfish sometimes! I have to get up in the morning! You don't!"

SUBJECT: THIS JOKE IS PANTS!

Paddy and Mick worked together, and were both laid off, so they went to the benefits office. When asked his profession Paddy answered "Panty Stitcher. I sew the elastic onto ladies cotton panties and thongs." The clerk looked up panty stitcher. Finding it classified as unskilled labour she gave him £45 a week unemployment benefit.

Mick was asked his occupation. "Diesel fitter" he replied. Since diesel fitter was a skilled job, the clerk gave Mick £90 a week.

When Paddy found out, he was furious. He stormed back in to find out why his friend was collecting double his pay. The clerk explained: "Panty stitchers are unskilled and diesel fitters are skilled labour."

"What skill?" yelled Paddy. "I sew the elastic on the panties and thongs. Mick puts them on his head and says "Yep, Diesel fitter."

RULE BRITANNIA! ONLY IN BRITAIN...

... can a pizza get to your house faster than an ambulance.

... do supermarkets make sick people walk all the way to the back of the shop to get their prescriptions while healthy people can buy cigarettes at the front.

... do people order double cheeseburgers, large fries and a DIET coke.

... do banks leave both doors open and chain the pens to the counters.

... do we leave cars worth thousands of pounds on the drive and lock our junk and cheap lawn mower in the garage.

... do we use answering machines to screen calls and then have call waiting so we won't miss a call from someone we didn't want to talk to in the first place.

... are there disabled parking places in front of a skating rink.

SUBJECT: BECKS IS DA MAN

David Beckham decides to go horse riding. Although he has had no previous experience, he skilfully mounts the horse and appears in complete command of the situation as the horse gallops along at a steady pace. Posh stands admiringly watching her husband. After a short time David becomes a little too casual, and begins to lose his grip in the saddle. He panics and grabs the horse around the neck shouting for it to stop.

Posh starts to scream and shout for someone to help her husband, as David has by this time slipped completely out of the saddle and is only saved from hitting the ground by the fact that he still has a grip on the horse's neck. David decides that his best chance is to leap away from the horse, but his foot has become entangled in one of the stirrups. As the horse gallops along David's head is banging on the ground and he is slipping into unconsciousness. Posh is now frantic and screams and screams for help!

Finally, fed up with it all, the Tesco Security Guard comes out and unplugs the horse.

BUSH AND THE DISASTER QUESTION

President George W Bush is visiting an elementary school one day and visits one of the classes. They are in the middle of a discussion related to words and their meanings. The teacher asks the President if he would like to lead the class in the discussion of the word 'tragedy'. So the illustrious leader asks the class for an example of tragedy.

One little boy stands up and offers, "If my best friend, who lives next door, is playing in the street and a car comes along and run him over, that would be a tragedy."

"No," says Bush, "although sad, that would be an accident."

A little girl raises her hand. "If a school bus carrying 50 children drove off a cliff, killing everyone involved, that would be a tragedy."

"I'm afraid not," explains Mr. President. "That's what we would call a great loss."

The room goes silent. No other children volunteer. President Bush searches the room. "Isn't there someone here who can give me an example of a tragedy?"

Finally, way in the back of the room, a small boy raises his hand. In a quiet voice he says, "If Air Force One – carrying President & Mrs Bush – was struck by a missile and blown to smithereens by a terrorist like Osama bin Laden, that would be a tragedy."

"Fantastic," exclaims Bush, "That's right. And can you tell me why that would be a tragedy?"

"Well," says the boy, "because it wouldn't be an accident and it certainly wouldn't be a loss."

SHORT AND SWEET

Q. Do you know how New Zealanders practice safe sex?
A. They spray-paint X's on the back of the sheep that kick.

Q. Why is divorce so expensive?
A. Because it's worth it.

Q: What do a Christmas tree and a priest have in common?
A: Their balls are just for decoration.

Q: What is the difference between "ooooooh" and "aaaaaaah"?
A: About three inches.

Q: What's the difference between purple and pink?
A: The grip.

Q: How do you find a blind man in a nudist colony?
A: It's not hard.

Q: What's the difference between a girlfriend and a wife?
A: 45 pounds.

Q: What's the difference between a boyfriend and a husband?
A: 45 minutes.

Q: Why do men find it difficult to make eye contact?
A: Breasts don't have eyes.

Q: If the dove is the bird of peace, what is the bird of true love?
A: The swallow.

Q: What is the difference between medium and rare?
A: Six inches is medium, eight inches is rare.

Q: Why do most women pay more attention to their appearance than improving their minds? A: Because most men are stupid, but few are blind.

THIS RABBIT IS NOT BAD — IT'S NOT RABBIT IT'S CHICKEN...

A hunter kills a deer and brings it home. He decides to clean and serve the deer meat for supper. He knows his kids are fussy eaters and won't eat it if they know what it is. So he doesn't tell them.

His little boy, Jimmy, keeps asking him, "What's for supper dad?"

"You'll see", he replies.

They start eating supper and his daughter keeps asking him what they are eating.

"Ok", says her dad, "Here's a hint. It's what your mother sometimes calls me."

His daughter screams. "Don't eat it Jimmy! It's an asshole!"

BIGGUS DICKUS

A man with a 25-inch penis goes to his doctor to complain that he is having a problem with this cumbersome instrument, and has had more than one complaint. "Doctor," he asks, in total frustration, "is there anything you can do for me?"

The doctor replies, "Medically son, there is nothing I can do. But, I do know this witch who may be able to help you." The doctor gives him directions to the witch.

The man calls upon the witch and tells his story. "Witch, my penis is 25 inches long and I need help. Can anything be done to help me? You are my only hope."

The witch stares in amazement, scratches her head, and then replies, "I think I may be able to help you with your problem. Do this. Go deep into the forest. There you will find a pond. In this pond, you will find a frog sitting on a log. This frog has magic powers. Say to the frog, 'Will you marry me?' When the frog says no, you will find five inches less to your problem."

The man's face lights up and he dashes off into the forest. He finds the frog and calls out to it, "Will you marry me?"

The frog looks at him dejectedly and replies, "No."

The man looks down and suddenly his penis is 5 inches shorter. "WOW," he screams out loud, "This is great!" His penis is still too long at 20 inches though, so he asks the frog to marry him again.

The frog rolls its eyes back in its head and screams back, "NO!"

The man feels another twitch in his penis, looks down and it is another 5 inches shorter. "This is fantastic!" He looks down at his penis again still 15 inches long and thinks for a moment. "Fifteen inches is still a monster, just a little less would be ideal."

Grinning, he looks across the pond and yells out, "Frog, will you marry me?"

The frog looks back across the pond shaking its head. "How many times do I have to tell you? No, no, a thousand times NO!"

OUT OF THE MOUTHS OF BABES...

A little girl walks into her parents' bathroom and sees her father fully naked for the first time. She is extremely curious, because he has equipment that she doesn't have. She asks, "What are those round things hanging there, daddy?"

Proudly, he replies, "Those, sweetheart, are God's Apples of Life. Without them we wouldn't be here."

Puzzled, she seeks her mummy out and tells her what daddy has said. After she tells her mum, her mummy asks, "Did he say anything about the dead branch they were hanging from?"

DOUBLE TROUBLE

After Quasimodo's death, the bishop of the cathedral of Notre Dame sent word through the streets of Paris that a new bell ringer was needed. The bishop decided that he would conduct the interviews personally, and went up into the belfry to begin the screening process. After observing several applicants demonstrate their skills, he was going to call it a day when an armless man approached him and announced that he was here to apply for the bell ringer's job.

The bishop was incredulous. "You have no arms!" he said.

"No matter", said the man, "Observe!"

He then began striking the bells with his face, producing a beautiful melody on the carillon. The bishop listened in astonishment, convinced that he had finally found a suitable replacement for Quasimodo. Suddenly, rushing forward to strike a bell, the armless man tripped and plunged headlong out of the belfry window, falling to his death in the street below. The stunned bishop rushed down to get to his side. When he reached to street, a crowd had gathered around the fallen figure, drawn by the beautiful music they had heard only moments before.

As they silently parted to let the bishop through, one of them asked, "Bishop, who was this man?"

"I don't know his name", the bishop sadly replied, "but his face rings a bell."

The following day, despite the sadness that weighed heavily on his heart due to the unfortunate death of the armless campanologist, the bishop continued his interviews for the bell ringer of Notre Dame.

The first man to approach him said, "Your Excellency, I am the brother of the poor, armless wretch who fell to his death from this very belfry yesterday. I pray that you honour his life by allowing me to replace him in this duty."

The bishop agreed to give the man an audition. As the armless man's brother stooped to pick up a mallet to strike the first bell, he groaned, clutched at his chest and died on the spot. Two monks, hearing the bishop's cries of grief at this second tragedy, rushed up the stairs to his side. "What has happened?" the first asked breathlessly. "Who is this man?"

"I don't know his name", sighed the distraught bishop, "but he's a dead ringer for his brother."

WISDOM

A saleswoman is driving toward home in Northern Arizona when she sees a Navajo woman hitchhiking. Because the trip has been long and quiet she stops the car and the Navajo woman climbs in. During their small talk, the Navajo woman glances surreptitiously at a brown bag on the front seat between them.

"If you're wondering what's in the bag," offers the saleswoman, "it's a bottle of wine. I got it for my husband."

The Navajo woman is silent for a while, then nods gravely and says, "Good trade."

BIG HEAD?

A huge muscular man walks into a bar and orders a beer. The bartender can't help but stare at the guy because in contrast to his large muscles, the man has a head that is the size of an orange. The bartender hands him the beer and says, "You know, I'm not gay but I want to compliment you on your physique, it's really phenomenal! But I have a question, why is your head so small?"

The big guy nods slowly. He's obviously fielded this question many times. "One day," he begins, "I was hunting and got lost in the woods. I heard someone crying for help. I followed the cries and they led me to a frog that was sitting next to a stream. 'Kiss me, kiss me and I will turn into a genie and grant you three wishes,' the frog said. I looked around to see if I was alone and gave the frog a kiss. WHOOSH! The frog turned into a beautiful, voluptuous woman. She said, 'Thank you. As a reward, you now have three wishes'.

"I looked down at my scrawny 115 pound body and said, 'I want a body like Arnold Schwarzenegger!' She nodded, snapped her fingers and WHOOSH!, I was so big that I ripped out of my clothes and was standing there naked! She then asked, 'What is your second wish?' I looked hungrily at her beautiful body and replied, 'I want to make passionate love with you by the stream.'

"She nodded, laid down and beckoned me. We screwed right there by the stream for hours! God, I was a sex machine. Afterwards, as we lay next to each other, sweating from our glorious lovemaking she whispered in my ear, 'You know you have one more wish, what will it be?'
"I looked at her and replied, 'How about a little head?'"

BEFORE YOU ASK, THIS HAS NOTHING TO DO WITH...

Johnny Cooper, a city boy, one day moved to the country and bought a donkey from an old farmer for £100. The farmer agreed to deliver the donkey, but the next day the farmer drove up and said, "Sorry son, but I have some bad news, the donkey died."

Johnny replied, "Well then, just give me my money back."

The farmer said, "Can't do that, sorry. I went and spent it already."

Johnny thought it over for a minute and said, "OK then, just unload the donkey."

The farmer asked, "What ya gonna do with him?"

"I'm going to raffle him off."

"You can't raffle off a dead donkey!"

"Of course I can. Watch me. I just won't tell anybody he is dead."

A month later the farmer meets up with Johnny Cooper and asks, "What happened with that dead donkey?"

"I raffled him off, as I told you I would. I sold 500 tickets at one pound a piece and made a profit of £400."

"Didn't anyone complain?"

" Just the guy who won. So I gave him his pound back."

FRIDAY HUMOUR

Some friends were sitting at the bar talking about their professions.

The first guy says, "I'm a Y. U.P. P. I. E. – you know, Young, Urban, Professional, Peaceful, Intelligent, Ecological."
The second guy says, "I'm a D. I. N. K. – you know, Double Income,

No Kids."

The third guy says, "I'm a R. U. B. – you know, Rich Urban, Biker."

They turn to one of the women and ask her, "What about you?"

She replies: "I'm a W. I. F. E. – you know, Wash, Iron, Fetch, Etc."
The second gal answers their question before they even ask it.

"B.I.T.C.H.," she says, leaving it at that.

"What's a B.I.T.C.H.?", they ask in unison.
"Babe In Total Control of Her own life."

SUBJECT: THE LOGICAL SEX (OR DON'T ANNOY A WOMAN WHEN SHE IS READING)

A couple go on vacation to a fishing resort in northern Minnesota. The husband likes to fish at the crack of dawn. The wife likes to read. One morning the husband returns after several hours of fishing and decides to take a nap. Although not familiar with the lake, the wife decides to take the boat out. She motors out a short distance, anchors and continues to read her book.

Along comes a game warden in his boat. He pulls up alongside the woman and says, "Good morning Ma'am. What are you doing?"

"Reading a book," she replies.

"You're in a restricted fishing area," he informs her.

"As long as it is not a restricted reading area, I should be fine then. I'm not fishing."
"The problem is that all the fishing equipment you need to fish with is in this boat. I'll have to take you in and write you up."

"That's ridiculous," she says. "If you do that, I'll have to phone the police and get them to charge you with rape."

"But I haven't even touched you," says the game warden, horrified.

"Ah, but the problem is that all the equipment you need..."

SUBJECT: SWALLOW THIS?

A little old lady answered a knock on the door one day, only to be confronted by a well-dressed young man carrying a vacuum cleaner. "Good morning," said the young man. "If I could take a couple minutes of your time, I would like to demonstrate the very latest in high-powered vacuum cleaners."

"Get lost!" said the old lady. "I haven't got any money," and she proceeded to close the door.

Quick as a flash, the young man wedged his foot in the door and pushed it wide open. "Don't be too hasty!" He said. "Not until you have at least seen my demonstration." With that, he slung a bucket of horse crap all over her hallway carpet. "If this vacuum cleaner does not remove all traces of this from your carpet, madam, I will personally eat the remainder."

"Well," she said, "I hope you've got a bloody good appetite, because the electricity was cut off this morning."

RUBBERS IN A FISH BOWL

Miss Bea, the church organist, was in her eighties and had never been married. She was much admired for her sweetness and kindness to all. The pastor came to call on her one afternoon early in the spring and she welcomed him into her Victorian parlour. She invited him to have a seat while she prepared a little tea.

As he sat facing her old pump organ, the young minister noticed a cut glass bowl sitting on top of it, filled with water. In the water floated, of all things, a condom. Imagine his shock and surprise. Imagine his curiosity! Surely Miss Bea had flipped or something...! When she returned with tea and cookies, they began to chat. The pastor tried to stifle his curiosity about the bowl of water and its strange floater, but soon it got  the better of him and he could resist no longer. "Miss Bea," he said, "I wonder if you would tell me about this?" pointing to the bowl.

"Oh, yes," she replied, "isn't it wonderful? I was walking into town last autumn and I found this little package on the ground. The directions said to put it on the organ, keep it wet and it would prevent disease. And, you know, I haven't had a cold all winter."

POPULARITY

A mortician was working late one night. It was his job to examine the dead bodies before they were sent off to be buried or cremated. As he examined the body of Mr Schwartz, he made an amazing discovery. Schwartz had the longest, thickest dick he had ever seen! "I'm sorry, Mr Schwartz," said the mortician, "but I can't send you off to be cremated with a tremendously huge penis like this. It has to be saved for posterity."

With that, the coroner used his scalpel to remove the dead man's privates. The coroner stuffed his prize into a briefcase and took it home. The first person he showed was his wife. "I have something to show you that you won't believe," he said, opening his briefcase.

"Oh, my God!" she screamed, "Schwartz is dead!"

SUITS YOU SIR

A woman stopped by unannounced at her recently married son's house. She rang the doorbell and walked in. She was shocked to see her daughter-in-law lying on the couch, totally naked. Soft music was playing and the aroma of perfume filled the room. "What are you doing?" she asked.

"I'm waiting for my husband to come home from work," the daughter-in-law answered. "This is my love dress."
"Love dress? But you're naked!"

"My husband loves me to wear this dress," she explained. "It excites him to no end. Every time he sees me in this dress, he instantly becomes romantic and ravages me for hours on end. He can't get enough of me."

The mother-in-law left. When she got home, she undressed, showered, put on her best perfume, dimmed the lights, put on a romantic CD and laid on the couch waiting for her husband to arrive. Finally, her husband came home. He walked in and saw her laying there so provocatively. "What are you doing?" he asked.

"This is my love dress," she whispered, sensually.
"Needs ironing," he said. "What's for dinner?"

FW: HEHEHE.....
THIS MADE ME LAUGH!

A duck walked into a bar and ordered a beer. The barman said, "Hey, you're a duck."

"Nothing wrong with your eyesight mate," observed the duck. "Yeah, but I mean, you can TALK!" said the barman.

"Guess what? Your ears are fine too", answered the duck, flapping up onto a stool. "Can I have a pint, please?"

The barman served the duck a beer and asked him, "So, what brings a duck like you to these parts?"

"Oh", said the duck, "I work on the building site across the road. We'll be here for a couple of weeks, and I'll most likely be in every lunch hour for a pint."

The duck slurped down his beer, wiggling his tail happily. Just as he said, all week the duck waddled over from his job at the building site and had a lunchtime pint.

The next week, the circus came to town on its annual round. The circus owner wandered in for a pint and the barman told him about the talking duck. "You should get that duck to join your circus," he said. "For a bit of a thank-you, I could fix you up with the duck, and you could make a lot of money. Everyone would love to see a talking duck, I think. Don't you?"

The circus man nodded his agreement excitely while sipping his beer, and the barman agreed to talk to the duck about the circus. The following day, the duck once again came in for his lunchtime pint. The barman said to the duck, "You know, the circus is in town and yesterday I was chatting to the owner about you. He's very interested in you."

"Really?" said the duck.

"Yeah, you could make a lot of money there. I can fix it up for you easily."

"Hang on," said the duck, "you did say a CIRCUS, didn't you?"
"That's right."

"One of those big tents. With a big pole in the middle."
"Yeah!"

"And they're made of canvas, aren't they?" asked the duck.

"Of course," replied the barman. "Look, I can get you a job there, starting tomorrow. Great money. The circus owner is dead keen on the idea."

The duck looked very puzzled. "But it's a TENT. Why would he want to hire a plasterer?"

AH, SWEEEET!

A little girl goes to the barber's with her father. She stands next to the barber chair, eating a chocolate muffin while her dad gets his hair cut.

The barber smiles at her and says, "Sweetheart, you're gonna get hair on your muffin."

"I know," she replies. "I'm gonna get tits, too."

WOMEN AND SEAMEN DON'T MIX

A male whale and a female whale were swimming off the coast of Japan when they noticed a whaling ship. The male whale recognised as the same ship that had harpooned his father many years earlier. He said to the female whale, "They're whalers, and they killed my dad. Let's both swim under the ship and blow out our air holes at the same time. That should cause the ship to turn over and sink."

They tried it and sure enough, the ship turned over and quickly sank. Soon however, the whales realised the sailors were swimming to the safety of the shore. The male whale was enraged that they were going to get away and told the female, "Let's swim after them and gobble them up before they reach the shore."

At this point he realised the female was becoming reluctant to follow him. "Look", she said, "I went along with the blow job, but I absolutely refuse to swallow seamen."

RADIO DAYS

This story occurred on the radio in Australia some time ago. One of the FM stations had a competition where they phoned someone up, asked them three personal questions, and then rang the person's spouse or partner and asked them the same three questions. If the answers were the same, the couple won a holiday. This time, the competition went like this:

Presenter: OK, first question, when was the last time you had sex?

Brian: Oooh, mate, well, about 8 this morning.

Presenter: And how long did it go on for Brian?

Brian: About 10 minutes...

Presenter: 10 minutes? Good one, and where did you do it mate?

Brian: Oooh, mate, I can't say that.

Presenter: There's a holiday to the Seychelles at stake here, Brian.

Brian : OK... OK... on the kitchen table.

Presenter: (and others in the room – much laughter) Good one, Brian, now is it OK for us to call your wife?

Brian : Yeah, alright.

Presenter: Hi, Sharelle, how are you?

Sharelle: Hi, good, thanks.

Presenter: We've got Brian on the other line, say hello.

Brian : Hi Sharelle.

Sharelle: Hi babe.

Presenter: Now Sharelle, we're going to ask you the same three questions we asked Brian, and if you give the same answers, you win a trip for two to the Seychelles.

Brian: Just tell the truth, honey.

Sharelle: OK.

Presenter: Sharelle, when was the last time you had sex?

Sharelle: Ooooh, nooo, I can't say that on the radio.

Brian: Sharelle, it doesn't matter, I've already told them.

Sharelle: OK... about 8 this morning, before Brian went to work.

Presenter: Good, nice start! Next question, how long did it go on for, Sharelle?

Sharelle: (giggling) About 12, maybe 15 minutes.

Co-presenter: That's close enough. Brian was just being a gentleman.

Presenter: OK, Sharelle, final question, where did you do it?

Sharelle: Oooh no, I can't say that, my mum could be listening, no way, no.

Presenter: There's a trip to the Seychelles on the line here.

Brian: Sharelle, I've already told them, so it doesn't matter anyway.

Sharelle: Oooh... Oooh, really? ... alright... up the arse!

... Radio silence ...

...Advert ...

Presenter: Sorry if anyone was offended before. We're live, and sometimes these things happen. We've given Brian and Sharelle the holiday. Now we'll take a music break...

IT TAKES ALLSORTS

Mr Cadbury and Ms Rowntree went off for the weekend. It was After Eight. She was from Quality Street, while he was a Fisherman's Friend. On the way they stopped at a Yorkie Bar. He had a Rum and Butter. She had a Wine Gum. He asked her name. She said 'Polo, I'm the one with the hole.' ('But I'm the one with the Nuts', he thought). Then he touched her Milky Way. They checked in and went straight to the bedroom. Mr Cadbury turned out the light for a bit of Black Magic. It wasn't long before he slipped his hand into her Snickers and felt the contrast of her Double Decker. Then he showed her his Curly Wurly. But Ms Rowntree wasn't keen as she already had a few Jelly Babies, so she let him take a trip down Bourneville Boulevard. He was pleased as he always fancied a bit of Fudge nudging. It was a Magic Moment as she let out of scream of Turkish Delight. When he came out his Fun Sized Mars Bar felt a bit Crunchie. She wanted more but he decided to take a Time Out. However, he noticed her Pink Wafers looked very appetising. So he did a Twirl and had a Picnic in her Sherbert. At the same time he gave her a Gob Stopper! Unfortunately Mr Cadbury had to go home to his wife Caramel. Sadly, he was soon to discover he had caught VD. It turns out Ms Rowntree had a Box of Assorted Creams. She really had been with Allsorts.

POKER?

A boy catches his mum and dad having sex. The boy is curious and says, "What are you two doing?"

The dad replies back, "We are playing poker, and your mum is the wild card."

About an hour later the father cannot find his son. He hears a noise in the bathroom and goes to check it out. He finds his son jacking off and says, "What in the hell are you doing?"

The boy replies, "I'm just playing poker."

Then the dad says, "How are you playing poker without a wild card?"

The boy replies, "With a hand like this, who needs a wild card?!"

SUBJECT: SILENCE IS GOLDEN

The priest said, "Sister, this is a silent monastery. You are welcome here as long as you like, but you may not speak until I direct you to do so."

Sister Mary Katherine lived in the monastery for five years before the priest said to her, "Sister Mary Katherine, you have been here for five years. You may speak two words."

Sister Mary Katherine said, "Hard bed."

"I'm sorry to hear that," the priest said, "We will get you a better bed."

After another five years, Sister Mary Katherine was called by the Priest. "You may say another two words, Sister Mary Katherine."

"Cold food," said Sister Mary Katherine and the priest assured her that the food would be warmer in the future.

On her 15th anniversary at the monastery, the priest again called Sister Mary Katherine into his office. "You may say two more words today."

"I quit," said Sister Mary Katherine.

"It's probably best", said the priest, "You've done fuck all but moan since you got here."

THE TRUTH ABOUT CREATION THAT THE BIBLE NEVER SAID A WORD ABOUT

In the beginning God created Eve. And she had 3 breasts. After three weeks in the garden, God came to visit Eve.
"How're things, Eve?" He asked.

"It is all so beautiful, God," she replied. "The sunrises and sunsets are breathtaking, the smells, the sights, everything is wonderful but I just have this one problem. It's these three breasts you've given me. The middle one pushes the other two out, and I am constantly knocking them with my arms, catching them on branches, snagging them on bushes – they're a real pain."

"That's a fair point," replied God, "but it was my first shot at that you know. I gave the animals, what, six? So I just figured you'd need half, but I see that you are right. I'll fix that up right away!" So, God reached down and removed the middle breast, tossing it into the bushes.

Three weeks passed and God once again visited Eve in the garden. "Well, Eve, how's my favourite creation?" He asked.

"Just fantastic," she replied, "but for one small oversight on your part.

You see, all the animals are paired off. The ewe has her ram, the cow has her bull, all the animals have a mate except me. I feel so alone."

God thought for a moment. "You know, Eve, you're right. How could I have overlooked this! You do need a mate and I will immediately create Man from a part of you! Now, let's see... where did I put that useless tit?"

AT THE MOVIES

Things you would never know without the movies...

- All beds have special L-shaped cover sheets which reach up to the armpit level of a woman but only to waist level on the man lying beside her.

- The ventilation system of any building is the perfect hiding place. No-one will ever think of looking for you in there, and you can travel to any other part of the building you want without any difficulty.

- Should you wish to pass yourself off as a German officer, it will not be necessary to speak the language. A German accent will do.

- A man will show no pain while taking the most ferocious beating, but will wince when a woman tries to clean his wounds.

- Kitchens don't have light switches. When entering a kitchen at night, you should open the fridge door and use that light instead.

- If staying in a haunted house, women should investigate any strange noises in their most revealing underwear.

- Cars that crash will always burst into flames.

- Wearing a vest or stripping to the waist can make a man invulnerable to bullets.

- If you find yourself caught up in a misunderstanding that could be cleared up quickly with a simple explanation, you must always keep your mouth shut.

- Any person waking from a nightmare will sit bolt upright and pant.

- A cough is usually the sign of a terminal illness.

- All bombs are fitted with electronic timing devices with large red digits so you know exactly when they're going to go off.

- When in love, it is customary to burst into song.

- When confronted by an evil international terrorist, sarcasm and wisecracks are your best weapons.

- One man shooting at 20 men has a better chance of killing them all than 20 men firing at one man have of even injuring him.

- Creepy music coming from a cemetery should always be investigated more closely.

- Most laptop computers are powerful enough to override the communication systems of any invading alien civilizations – who all use American operating systems.

- Freelance helicopter pilots are always eager to accept bookings from international terrorist organizations, even though the job will require them to shoot total strangers and will end in their own certain death as the helicopter explodes in a ball of flames.

- Most people keep a scrapbook of newspaper clippings – especially if one of their family or friends died in a strange boating accident.

- All computer disks will work in all computers, regardless of software or operating systems.

- Police Departments give their officers personality tests to make sure they are deliberately assigned a partner who is their total opposite.

- When they are alone, all foreigners prefer to speak English to each other.

- Action heroes never face charges for manslaughter or criminal damage despite laying entire cities to waste by their actions.

- You can always find a chainsaw when you need one.

- Any lock can be picked by a credit card or a paper clip in seconds – unless it is the door to a burning building with a child trapped inside.

- You can tell if somebody is British because they will be wearing a bow tie.

- When driving a car, it is normal to look not at the road but at the person sitting beside you (or in the back seat) for the entire journey.

- An electric fence powerful enough to kill a dinosaur will cause no lasting damage to an 8 year old child.

- Having a job of any kind will make fathers forget their son's eighth birthday.

- Honest and hardworking policemen are traditionally gunned down three days before their retirement.

- If you are blonde and pretty, it is possible to become a world expert in Nuclear Fission at age 22.

- The more a man and a woman hate each other, the more likely they will fall in love.

- If being chased through town, you can usually take cover in a passing St Patrick's Day parade – at any time of the year.

- All grocery shopping bag contain at least one stick of French bread.

- It's easy for anyone to land a plane, providing there is someone in the control tower to talk you down.

- Once applied, lipstick will never rub off – even when scuba diving.

- You're likely to survive any battle in any war unless you make the mistake of showing someone a picture of your sweetheart back home.

- The Eiffel Tower can be seen from any window of any building in Paris.

- People never finish their drinks.

- The chief of police is always black.

- When paying for a taxi, never look at your wallet as you take out a note. Just grab one at random and hand it over. It will always be the exact fare.

TIGER WOODS' EX

A couple were on their honeymoon, lying in bed, about ready to consummate their marriage, when the new bride says to the husband, 'I have a confession to make. I'm not a virgin.'

The husband replies, 'That's no surprise in this day and age.' The wife continues,

'Yeah, I've been with one guy.'

'Oh yeah? Who was the guy?'

'Tiger Woods.'

'Tiger Woods, the golfer?'

'Yeah.'

'Well he's rich, famous and handsome. I can see why you went to bed with him.'

The husband and wife then made passionate love. When they finished, the husband got up and walked to the telephone. "What are you doing?" asked the wife.

The husband said, "I'm going to call room service for some food."
"Tiger wouldn't do that."

"Oh yeah? What would Tiger do?"

"He'd come back to bed and do it a second time."

The husband put down the phone and went back to bed, and made love to his wife a second time. When they finished, he got up again and went over to the phone. "What are you doing?" She asked.

The husband said, "I'm still hungry, so I was going to phone room service to order some food."

"Tiger wouldn't do that."

"Oh yeah? What would Tiger do?"

"He'd come back to bed and do it one more time."

The guy slammed down the phone and went back to bed, and made love to his wife one more time. When they finally finished, he was gasping for air, and glistening with sweat. He dragged himself over to the phone and started to dial. His wife asked, "Are you calling room service?"

"No! I'm calling Tiger Woods to find out what the par is for this damn hole."

FOURRRRRR!!!!!

A LITTLE OFFICE PRAYER (I NEED IT!)

Dear Lord, grant me the serenity to accept the things I cannot change, the courage to change the things I cannot accept, and the wisdom to hide the bodies of those people I had to kill today because they annoyed me. Also help me to be careful of the toes I step on today, as they may be connected to the arse that I might have to kiss tomorrow. Help me to always give 100% at work: 12% on Monday, 23% on Tuesday, 40% on Wednesday, 20% on Thursday, and 5% on Friday. Help me to remember that when I'm having a really bad day, and it seems that people are trying to piss me off, that it takes 42 muscles to frown and only four to extend my fingers and tell them to F off. Amen.

YEP, YOU'RE OLD ENOUGH FOR THIS ONE!!!

Congratulations are in order if you lived as a child in the 60s, 70s or even early 80s. Looking back, it's hard to believe that we have lived as long as we have...

As children, we would ride in cars with no seat belts or air bags. Our baby cribs were covered with brightly-coloured lead-based paint. We had no childproof lids on medicine bottles, doors, or cabinets, and when we rode our bikes, we had no helmets. (Not to mention hitchhiking as a young kid!) We drank water from the garden hose and not from a bottle. We would spend hours building our go-carts out of scraps, and then we'd ride down the hill only to find out we forgot the brakes. After running into the bushes a few times, we would learn to solve the problem. We would leave home in the morning and play all day as long as we were back before dinner time, and no one was able to reach us all day because we didn't have mobile phones.

We played dodgeball and sometimes the ball would really hurt. We got cut and broke bones and broke teeth, and there were no lawsuits from these accidents. They were just... accidents. No one was to blame but us. Remember accidents? We had fights and punched each other and got black and blue and learned to get over it. We ate cupcakes, bread and butter, and drank sugared soft drinks but, we were never overweight. We shared one soft drink with four friends, from one bottle and no one died from this.

We did not have Playstations, Nintendo 64s, X-Boxes, video games, 99 channels on pay TV, videos or DVDs, surround sound, Personal Computers, Internet chat rooms ... we had friends. We went outside and found them. We rode bikes or walked to a friend's home and knocked on the door, or rung the bell, or just walked in and talked to them. Imagine such a thing. Without asking a parent! By ourselves! Out there in the cold cruel world! Without a guardian! How did we do it?

We made up games with sticks and tennis balls, and ate worms, and although we were told it would happen, we did not put out very many eyes, nor did the worms live inside us forever. We played footy down the park and not everyone got picked to play. Those who didn't had to learn to deal with disappointment. Some students weren't as smart as others, so they failed a grade, and some were even held back to repeat the same grade. Tests were not adjusted for any reason, and exams were tough — a good mark meant you really were good, not that you just showed up. Our actions were our own. Consequences were expected. There was no-one to hide behind. The idea of a parent bailing us out if we broke a law was unheard of. Much more likely, we'd get punished by them too. They actually sided with the law — imagine that!

Our generation has produced some of the best risk-takers and problem solvers and inventors — ever. The past 50 years has been an explosion of innovation and new ideas. We had freedom, failure, success and responsibility, and we learned how to deal with it all. And you're one of us. Congratulations! Please pass this on to others who had the luck to grow up as real kids, before greedy lawyers and grand-standing politicians regulated our lives out of all existence for our own 'good'.

CHRISTMAS MYTH

One particular Christmas season a long time ago, Santa was getting ready for his annual trip, but there were problems everywhere. Four of his elves got sick and the trainee elves did not produce the toys as fast as the regular ones, so he was beginning to feel the pressure of being behind schedule. Then Mrs. Claus told Santa that her mum was coming to visit. This stressed Santa even more. When he went to harness the reindeer, he found that three of them were about to give birth and two had jumped the fence and were out, heaven knows where. More stress. Then when he began to load the sleigh, one of the boards cracked and the toy-bag fell to the ground and scattered the toys.

Frustrated, Santa went into the house for a cup of coffee and a shot of whiskey. When he went to the cupboard, he discovered that the elves had hid the liquor and there was nothing to drink. In his frustration, he accidentally dropped the coffeepot and it broke into hundreds of little pieces all over the kitchen floor. He went to get the broom and found that mice had eaten the straw it was made from.

Just then the doorbell rang and Santa cursed on his way to the door. He opened the door and there was a little angel with a great big Christmas tree. The angel said, very cheerfully, "Merry Christmas, Santa. Isn't it just a lovely day? I have a beautiful tree for you. Isn't it just a lovely tree? Where would you like me to stick it?"

Thus began the tradition of the little angel on top of the Christmas tree.

WHAT WE HAVE HERE IS A FAILURE TO COMMUNICATE

A man walked into a supermarket with his zip down. One of the female cashiers walked up to him and said, "Your barracks door is open!" This is not a phrase men usually use, so he went on his way looking a bit puzzled. When he had just about done his shopping, a man came up to him and said, "Your fly is open!" Our man zipped it up and finished his shopping.

He then intentionally got into the queue to pay the woman who had told him about 'his barracks door'. He was planning to have a little fun with her on his way out. When he reached the till, he said to her, "When you saw my barracks door open, did you see a soldier standing to attention in there?"

The woman thought for a moment then said, "No, no, I didn't. All I saw was a disabled veteran squatting glumly on a pair of duffel bags!"

SIGNS SEEN AT THE WASHINGTON PEACE DEMONSTRATION

1) (On the American flag) These colours don't run the world
2) One nation under surveillance
3) How did our oil get under their sand?

4) Go Solar, not Ballistic

5) What would Jesus bomb?

6) Start Drafting SUV Drivers Now

7) Don't blame me, I voted with the majority

8) Buck Fush!

9) It's NUCLEAR not NUCULAR, you idiot!

10) Patriots are idiots – Matriarchy Now!

11) Resistance is Fertile

12) (Pictures of sheep carrying flags) Stop Mad Sheep Disease Now

13) (UFW sign) Pick Fruit, not Fights

14) (On a five year old) More Candy, Less War

15) Say can you see my democracy?

16) (Pictures of Bush, Cheney and Rumsfeld) The Asses of Evil

17) It's the oil, stupid

18) War is expensive, Peace is priceless

19) Read between the Pipelines

20) No More BuSh

21) Smart weapons, Dumb president

22) The only thing we have to fear is Bush himself

23) How many Lives per Gallon?

24) Peace Takes Brains

25) Anything War can do, Peace can do better

26) Negotiation Not Annihilation

27) Make touchdowns, not war – Go Raiders!

28) Another patriot for peace

29) Don't do it, George, Dad will still love you

30) Power to the Peaceful

31) The last time we listened to a Bush, we wandered in the desert for 40 years

MAN, THIS MUST BE THE STUPIDEST JOKE EVER

Count Dracula is on the pull in Glasgow. He spends the night drinking glasses of Bloody Mary in various clubs and biting on unsuspecting women's necks. Sometime before sunrise, he heads for home, wandering along Argyle Street. Suddenly... SMACK! He is hit on the back of the head. He looks round and sees nothing, but at his feet there is a small sausage roll. "Hmm," he thinks. "What's going on here?"

A few yards further on and... BANG. Smacked on the back of the head again! He whirls round as quickly as he can, but there's nothing but a small triangular sandwich with the crusts cut off lying there on the ground. How odd! He continues once again, but he's only a few yards further along the street when... CRASH! Smacked on the back of the head yet again! He whirls round as quickly as he can again, but still nothing. He's getting really angry now, and only is half-surprised to notice a chicken drumstick lying on the ground.

He stands and peers into the darkness of the night. Nothing. He walks a few yards further, and feels a tap on the shoulder. With a swirl of his cape and a cloud of mist, he turns as fast as he can. Then he feels a sharp pain in his heart, and falls to the ground clutching his chest, which is punctured by a small wooden cocktail stick laden with a chunk of cheese and cube of pineapple. On the ground dying, he looks up and sees a young female. With his last breath he gasps, "Who the fuck are you?"

She replies, "I'm Buffet, the Vampire Slayer."

DISGUSTING!

A bunch of first-year medical students were receiving their first anatomy class with a real dead human body. They all gathered around the surgery table with the body covered with a white sheet. The professor started the class by telling them, "It is absolutely necessary to have two important qualities as a Doctor of Medicine. The first has to be that you're not disgusted by anything involving the human body." As an example, the professor pulled back the sheet, rolled the body over and stuck his finger up the corpse's arse, withdrew it, and then stuck it in his mouth. "Go ahead and do the same thing," he told his students.

The students freaked out, hesitated for several minutes, but eventually took turns sticking a finger up the dead body's rectum and then sucking on it. When everyone had finished, and they were all looking queasy, the professor looked at them and said, "The second most important quality is observation. I inserted my middle finger and sucked on my index finger. Now learn to pay attention!"

THE KEY TO A GOOD
RELATIONSHIP IS FEAR

A couple was celebrating their golden wedding anniversary. Their domestic tranquillity had long been the talk of the town and a local newspaper reporter was inquiring as to the secret of their long and happy marriage. "Well, it dates back to our honeymoon," explained the man.

"We visited the Grand Canyon and took a trip down to the bottom of the canyon by pack mule. We hadn't gone too far when my wife's mule stumbled. My wife quietly said, 'That's once.' We proceeded a little further and the mule stumbled again. Once more my wife quietly said, 'That's twice.'

"We hadn't gone a half-mile further when the mule stumbled the third time. My wife quietly removed a revolver from her purse and shot the mule dead. I started an angry protest over her treatment of the mule, when she looked at me, and quietly said, 'That's once...'"

ELEMENTARY, MY DEAR WATSON

Sherlock Holmes and Dr. Watson were on a camping trip. They had a bottle of wine and went to bed. A couple hours later Holmes woke up and said, "Watson, look up and tell me what you see."

Watson was silent a minute then said, "Dash it Holmes, I just see millions and millions of stars."

Holmes replied "And what does that tell you, Watson?"

Watson said, "Well, let me see. Ah, astrologically I see Leo is in Saturn. Astronomically I see that there are millions of galaxies and potentially billions of planets. Meteorologically I predict it will be a beautiful day tomorrow. Theologically I see God is all powerful and we are small and insignificant."

After a few moments of disgusted silence Holmes said, "Watson, you pillock! Some bastard has stolen our tent."

A BIT LONG, BUT SOOOOO NICE

A young man called Derrick wanted to purchase a gift for his new sweetheart's Christmas present. As they had not been dating for very long, after careful consideration he decided that a pair of gloves would strike the right note, not too romantic and not too personal. Accompanied by his sweetheart's sister, he went to Harrods and bought a dainty pair of white gloves. The sister purchased a pair of panties for herself at the same time. During the wrapping the shop assistant mixed up the two items – the sister got the gloves and Derrick got the panties. Without checking the contents, he sealed the package and sent it to his sweetheart with the following note:

Dear Maria,

I chose these because I noticed that you are not in the habit of wearing any when we go out in the evening. If it had not been for your sister, I would have chosen the long ones with the buttons, but she wears short ones that are easier to remove. These are a delicate shade, but the lady I bought them from showed me the pair that she had been wearing for the past three weeks and they were hardly soiled at all. I had her try yours on for me and she looked really smart in them even though they were a little tight on her. She also told me that her pair rubs her ring which helps keep it clean and shiny – in fact she has not needed to wash it since she had begun wearing them.

I wish I were there to put them on for you for the first time, as no doubt many other hands will touch them before I have a chance to see you again. When you take them off, remember to blow into them before putting them away, as they will naturally be a little damp from wearing. Just think how many times my lips will kiss them during the coming year. I hope that you will wear them for me on Friday night.

All my love, Derrick.

P.S. The latest style is to wear them folded down with a little fur showing.

EARTHQUAKE IN WALES

A MAJOR EARTHQUAKE measuring 4.8 on the Richter scale hit in the early hours of Friday 24th January 2003, epicentered on Swansea, South Wales. Victims could be seen wandering aimlessly muttering, "How be?", "Tidy," and "Can't fault it, but..." The earthquake decimated the area, causing approximately £30 worth of damage. Several price-less collections of mementos from the Balearics and Spanish Costas were damaged. Three areas of historic and scientifically significant burnt out cars were disturbed. Many were woken well before their giro arrived and thousands are still confused and bewildered, trying to come to terms with the fact that something interesting had hap-pened. One resident, Sara-Angharad Davies, a 15-year-old mother said, "It was such a shock, little Chardonnay-Mercedes came running into my bedroom crying. My youngest two, Tyler-Morgan and Me-gan-Storm, slept through it. I was still shaking when I was watch-ing Kilroy the next morning." Apparently, looting, muggings and car crime have carried on as normal however. The British Red Cross have so far managed to ship 4000 crates of Sunny Delight to the area to help the stricken masses. Rescue workers are still searching through the rubble and have found large quantities of personal belongings including benefit books, jewellery from Elizabeth Duke at Argos, and bone china from Poundland.

THIS IS SOOOOOOOOOO TRUE!

The perfect day For HER

8.15 Wake up to hugs and kisses
8.30 Weigh in 2kg lighter than yesterday
8.45 Breakfast in bed – freshly squeezed orange juice and croissants; open presents – expensive jewellery chosen by thoughtful partner
9.15 Soothing hot bath with frangipani bath oil
10.00 Light work out at club with handsome, funny personal trainer
10.30 Facial, manicure, shampoo, condition, blow dry
12.00 Lunch with best friend at fashionable outdoor café
12.45 Catch sight of partner's ex and notice she has gained 7kg
1.00 Shopping with friends, unlimited credit
3.00 Nap
4.00 Three dozen roses delivered by florist, card from secret admirer
4.15 Light work-out at club, followed by massage from strong but handsome hunk who says he rarely gets to work on such a perfect body
5.30 Choose outfit from expensive designer wardrobe, parade before full-length mirror
7.30 Candlelit dinner for two followed by dancing, with compliments received from other diners/dancers
10.00 Hot shower (alone)
10.15 Carried to a bed laden with freshly ironed, crisp, new, white linen
11.00 Pillow talk, light touching and cuddling
11.15 Fall asleep in his big strong arms

For HIM

6.00 Alarm
6.15 Blow job
6.30 Massive satisfying dump while reading the sports section
7.00 Breakfast – rump steak, eggs, coffee, toast, all cooked by naked buxom wench
7.30 Limo arrives
7.45 Several Jack Daniels and Cokes en-route to airport
9.15 Flight in personal Lear jet
9.30 Limo to Riverside Oaks Golf Club (blow job en-route)
9.45 Play front nine (2 under)
11.45 Lunch – two dozen oysters, three crown lagers, a bottle of Dom Perignon

12.15 Blow job
12.30 Play back nine (4 under)
2.15 Limo back to the airport (several JDs and Cokes)
2.30 Fly to Great Barrier Reef
3.30 Late afternoon fishing excursion with all-female crew (all nude)
4.30 Land world record Marlin (1234lbs) – on light tackle
5.00 Fly home, massage and hand job by naked Elle McPherson
6.45 Shit, shower and shave
7.00 Watch news: Michael Jackson assassinated; Denise Van Outen and Melanie Sykes animal farm video released and authenticated
7.30 Dinner – lobster appetisers, Dom Perignon (1953), big juicy filler steak, bottle of Grange
9.00 Napoleon brandy and Cohuna cigar in front of wall-size TV showing the highlights of England thrashing the Aussies
9.30 Sex with three hot, 19yr old bisexual girls
11.00 Massage and jacuzzi with tasty pizza snacks and a cleansing ale
11.30 Blow-job
11.45 In bed alone
11.50 A 12-second fart which changes note four times and forces the dog to leave the room

THE OLD MAN, THE BOY AND THE DONKEY

An old man, a boy and a donkey were going to town. The boy rode on the donkey and the old man walked. As they went along, they passed some people who remarked it was a shame the old man was walking and the boy was riding. The man and the boy thought maybe the critics were right, so they changed positions.

Later, they passed some people who remarked it was a shame the old man was making the little boy walk. They then decided they both would walk! Soon they passed some more people who thought they were stupid to walk when they had a decent donkey to ride, so they both rode the donkey. Then they passed some people who shamed them by saying how awful it was to put such a load on a poor donkey. The boy and man said they were probably right, so they decided to carry the donkey. As they crossed the bridge, they lost their grip on the animal and it fell into the river and drowned.

The moral of this story? If you try to please everyone, you might as well kiss your ass good-bye.

BAR FLIES

Two peanuts walk into a bar. One was a salted.

A jump-lead walks into a bar. The barman says, "I'll serve you, but don't start anything."

A catholic priest, a rabbi and a voodoo Houngan walk into a bar. The barman says, "What is this, some sort of joke?"

A sandwich walks into a bar. The barman says, "Sorry we don't serve food in here."

A dyslexic man walks into a bra.

A man walks into a bar with a roll of tarmac under his arm and says, "A pint please, and one for the road."

A baby seal walks into a club. What a damn tragedy.

GOOD DOG

A man takes his Rottweiler to the vet.

"My dog's cross-eyed," the man says. "Is there anything you can do for him?"

"Well," says the vet, "let's have a look at him"

The vet picks the dog up and examines his eyes, then checks his teeth. Finally he says, "I'm going to have to put him down."

The man is stricken. "What? Just because he's cross-eyed?"

"No," says the vet. "Because my arms are really starting to hurt."

SNAPPIES

Apparently, one in five people in the world are Chinese. And there are five people in my family, so it must be one of them. It's either my mum or my dad. Or my older brother Colin. Or my younger brother Fung-Jei. But I reckon it's Colin.

I went to buy some camouflage trousers the other day, but I couldn't find any.
I went to the butchers the other day and I bet him fifty quid that he couldn't reach the meat off the top shelf. He declined, saying that the steaks were too high.

My friend drowned in a bowl of muesli. He was pulled in by a strong currant.

I went to a seafood disco last week, but I pulled a muscle.

WAR OF THE SEXES

Q: What do you call an intelligent, good looking, sensitive man?
A: A rumour.

On the wall in the ladies' room: "My husband follows me everywhere..."
Written just below it: "No I do not!"

He said: "Shall we try swapping positions tonight?"
She said: "That's a good idea... you stand by the ironing board while I'll sit on the sofa and fart."

He said: "What have you been doing with all the grocery money I gave you?"
She said: "Turn sideways and look in the mirror."

Q: What had three legs and lived on a farm? A: The McCartneys.

BAR BRAWL

An Englishman, an Aussie and a South African are in a bar one night, having beer. All of a sudden the South African downs his beer, throws his glass in the air, pulls out a gun, shoots the glass to pieces and says, "In Sath Effrika our glasses are so cheap that we don't need to drink from the same one twice."

The Aussie, obviously impressed by this, drinks his beer, throws his glass into the air, pulls out his gun, shoots the glass to pieces and says, "Well mate, in Straaaaailia we have so much sand to make our glasses out of that we don't need to drink out of the same glass twice either."

The Englishman, cool as a cucumber, picks up his beer, drinks it, throws his glass into the air, pulls out his gun, and shoots the South African and the Australian stone dead. He turns to the bartender, "In London, we have so many South Africans and Australians that we don't need to drink with the same ones twice."

DID YOU KNOW?

- There are 3 billion women who don't look like supermodels and ONLY A FEW DOZEN WHO DO.

- Marilyn Monroe was a size 12 (that's UK size 16).

- If Barbie was a real woman, she'd have to walk on all fours due to her proportions.

- The average Western woman weighs 144 lbs (10 stone 4lb, 72kg) and wears between a size 12 and 14 (UK size 16-18).

- One out of every four college-aged women has an eating disorder.

- The models in the magazines are airbrushed – THEY DON'T LOOK LIKE THAT!

- A psychological study in 1995 found that three minutes spent looking at women in a fashion magazine caused 70% of women to feel depressed, guilty and shameful.

- 20 years ago, on average, models weighed 8% less than the average woman. Today they weigh 23% less.

THE ORIGINS OF THE WORD "SHIT"

In the 16th and 17th centuries, before the invention of commercial fertiliser, everything had to be transported by ship. Therefore, large shipments of manure were common. It was shipped dry, because in dry form it weighed a lot less than when wet, but once water (at sea) hit it, it not only became heavier, but the process of fermentation began again, of which a by-product is methane gas.

As the stuff was stored below decks in bundles, you can see what could (and did sometimes) happen. Methane would begin to build up below decks and the first time someone went below at night with a lantern, BOOOOM! Several ships were destroyed in this manner before it was determined just what was happening.

After that, the bundles of manure were always stamped with the term 'Ship High In Transit' on them which meant for the sailors to stow it high enough off the lower decks so that any water that came into the hold would not touch this volatile cargo and start the production of methane. Thus evolved the term 'S.H.I.T.', which has come down through the centuries and is in use to this very day. You probably did not know the true history of this word. Neither did I.

I always thought it was a golf term.

(NOTE: As you might expect, this history is actually complete shit. The word is over a thousand years old, and comes from the ancient Anglo-Saxon term "scittan", referring to cows with diarrhoea. The word "fuck" is similarly ancient. Besides which, the one thing that almost nowhere in the world is short of is shit – the damn stuff is everywhere – and if methane was heavier than air, you'd never smell farts. So who said joke books never teach you anything?)

THIS IS HOW SHIT HAPPENS

In The Beginning was The Plan. Then came the Assumptions, And the Assumptions were without form, As the Plan was without substance. The darkness fell upon the face of the workers, And they spake amongst themselves, saying "It is a crock of shit, and it stinketh."

And the workers went unto their Supervisors and spake unto them, "It is but a pile of the very worst dung, and none of us may face the odour thereof."

And the Supervisors went unto their Managers and spake unto them, "It is a container of excrement and it is very strong, such that none may abide by it."

And the Managers went unto their Directors crying unto them, "It is a vessel of fertiliser, and none may abide its strength."

And the Directors spake amongst themselves, saying one unto another, "It contains that which aids plant growth, and it is very strong." And the Directors went unto the Vice Presidents and spake unto them, "It doth promote growth, and is very powerful."

And the Vice Presidents went unto the President and spake unto him, "This new Plan will powerfully promote the growth of this Company."

And the President looked upon the Plan, and saw that it was good, and the Plan became Policy.

FRANCE: FOR AMERICANS AND ANYONE ELSE WHO KNOWS THE TRUTH

The following advisory for American travellers heading for France was compiled from information provided by the U.S. State Department, the Central Intelligence Agency, the U.S. Chamber of Commerce, the Food and Drug Administration, the Centre for Disease Control, the ECHELON communications interception system, and some very expensive spy satellites that the French don't know about. It is intended as a guide for American travellers only, and no guarantee of accuracy is ensured or intended.

General overview

France is a medium-sized foreign country situated on the continent of Europe. It is bounded by Germany, Switzerland and some smaller places of no particular consequence or shopping opportunities. France is a very old country with many treasures such as the Louvre and EuroDisney. Among its contributions to Western civilization are champagne, Camembert cheese, the guillotine, and body odour. Although France likes to think of itself as a modern nation, air conditioning is little used and it is next to impossible to get decent Mexican food. One continuing exasperation for American visitors is that the people wilfully persist in speaking French, although many will speak English if shouted at repeatedly.

The people

France has a population of 54 million people, most of whom drink and smoke a great deal, drive like lunatics, are dangerously over-sexed and have no concept of standing patiently in line. Men sometimes have girls' names like Marie and they kiss each other when they hand out medals. American travellers are advised to travel in groups and to wear baseball caps and colourful pants for easier mutual recognition.

Safety

In general, France is a safe destination, although travellers are advised that France is occasionally invaded by Germany. By tradition, the French surrender more or less at once and, apart from a temporary shortage of Scotch whisky and increased difficulty in getting baseball scores and stock market prices, life for the visitors generally goes on much as before. A tunnel connecting France to Britain beneath the English Channel has been opened in recent years to make it easier for the French government to flee to London.

History

France was discovered by Charlemagne in the Dark Ages. Other important historical figures are Louis XIV, Marie Antoinette, Joan of Arc, Jacques Cousteau, and Charles de Gaulle, who was President for many years before becoming an airport.

Government

The French form of government is democratic but noisy. Elections are held more or less continuously and always result in a runoff. Parliament's principal preoccupations are setting off atomic bombs in the South Pacific and acting indignant when anyone complains. According to the most up-to-date State Department intelligence, the current President is someone named Jacques or Francois or Claude or something. Further information is not available at this time.

Economy
France's principal exports, in order of importance to the economy, are wine, nuclear weapons, perfume, guided missiles, champagne, high-calibre weaponry, grenade launchers, land mines, tanks, attack aircraft, miscellaneous armaments and cheese.

Conclusion
France enjoys a rich history, a picturesque and varied landscape and a temperate climate. In short, it would be a very nice country if French people didn't inhabit it, and it wasn't still radioactive from all the nuclear tests they run. Remember no one ordered you to go abroad. Personally, we always take our vacation in Florida, and you are advised to do the same.

I WANNA FEEL LIKE A WOMAN, LOL

A transatlantic plane is passing through a severe storm. The turbulence is awful, and things go from bad to worse when one wing is struck by lightning. One woman in particular loses it. Screaming, she stands up in the front of the plane. "I'm too young to die," she wails. "If I'm going to die, I want my last minutes on earth to be memorable! Is there anyone on this plane who can make me feel like a woman?"

For a moment there is silence. Everyone has forgotten their own peril. They all stare, riveted, at the terrified woman in the front of the plane. Then an Italian man stands up in the rear of the plane. He is gorgeous tall, well built, with dark brown hair and hazel eyes. He starts to walk slowly up the aisle, unbuttoning his shirt, one button at a time. He removes his shirt, muscles rippling across his chest. The woman gasps, and he leans down to her ear and whispers, "Iron this and get me something to eat."

CORPORATE LESSON 4

Case: A man is getting into the shower just as his wife is getting out, when the doorbell rings. After a few seconds of arguing over which one should go and answer the doorbell, the wife gives up, quickly wraps herself up in a towel and runs downstairs. When she opens the door, there stands Bob, the next door neighbour.

Before she says a word, Bob says, "I'll give you £800 to drop that towel you have on." After thinking for a moment, the woman drops her towel and stands naked in front of Bob. After a few seconds, Bob hands her £800 and leaves. Confused, but excited about her good fortune, the woman wraps back up in the towel and goes back upstairs.

When she gets back to the bathroom, her husband asks from

the shower, "Who was that?"

"It was Bob the next door neighbour," she replies.

"Great," the husband says. "Did he say anything about the £800 he owes me?"

Analysis: If you share critical information pertaining to credit and risk in time with your stakeholders, you may be in a position to prevent avoidable exposure.
you need.

PIECES OF WISDOM WE COULDN'T POSSIBLY LIVE WITHOUT...

- The one word that clearly pin-points the reason why the human race has not achieved, and never will achieve its full potential is the word 'meetings'.

- Work is good, but it's not important enough to die for. Do not confuse your career with your life.

- No matter what happens, somebody will find a way to take it too seriously.

- The most powerful force in the universe is gossip.

- The one thing that unites all human beings, regardless of age, gender, religion, economic status or ethnic background, is that, deep down inside, we ALL believe that we are above average drivers.

- Remember that a lone amateur built the Ark. A large group of professionals built the Titanic.

- The five most essential words for a healthy, vital relationship are "I apologise," and "You are right."

- When you make a mistake, make amends immediately. If you have to eat shit, it is more pleasant to do it while it's still warm.

- Learn to pick your battles. Ask yourself, "Will this matter one year from now? How about one month? One week? One day?"

- Be really nice to your family and friends. You never know when you are going to need them to empty your bedpan.

AMERICA

A British doctor says, "Medicine in my country is so advanced that we can take a brain out of one man, put it in another and have him looking for work in six weeks."

A German doctor says, "That's nothing. We can take a brain out of one person, put it in another and have him preparing for war in four weeks."

An American doctor, not to be outdone, says, "You guys are way behind. We took a man with no brain out of Texas and put him in the White House, and now half the country is looking for work, and the other half is preparing for war."

DWARFISM

The seven dwarves are down in the mines when there is a cave-in. Snow White runs to the entrance and yells down to them. In the distance, a voice shouts out, "West Ham are good enough to win the League!"

Snow White sighs and says, "Well, at least Dopey's alive!"

HEY GRAMPS!

A man was walking down the street when he noticed his grandfather sitting on the porch in a rocking chair, naked from the waist down.

"Grandpa, what are you doing?" he exclaimed. The old man looked off into the distance without replying. "Grandpa, what are you doing sitting out here without anything on below the waist?" he asked him again.

"Well," the old man replied reluctantly, "last week I sat out here without a shirt on and got a stiff neck. This is your Grandma's idea!"

IN THE SHOWER

HOW TO SHOWER LIKE A WOMAN

Take off clothing and place it in the sectioned laundry hamper according to lights and darks.

Walk into bathroom wearing long dressing gown. If you see your husband along the way, cover up any exposed areas.

Look at womanly physique in the mirror. Make a mental note, must do more sit ups.

Get in the shower.

Use face cloth, arm cloth, leg cloth, long loofah, wide loofah and pumice stone.

Wash your hair with cucumber and sage shampoo with 43 added vitamins.

Wash your hair again to make sure it's clean.

Condition your hair with grapefruit mint conditioner enhanced with natural avocado oil.

Leave for 15 minutes.

Wash your face with crushed apricot kernel facial scrub for 14 minutes until face is red.

Wash the entire rest of body with ginger nut and Jaffa cake body wash.

Rinse conditioner off hair, making sure that it is all gone.
Shave armpits and legs.

Consider shaving bikini line but decide to get it waxed instead.

Scream loudly when husband flushes the toilet and you lose water pressure.

Turn off shower, squeegee off all the wet surfaces in the shower and spray mould with Domestos.

Get out of the shower.

Dry with a towel the size of a small country.

Wrap hair in super absorbent second towel.

Check entire body for any signs of a zit.

Tweeze hairs.

Return to the bedroom wearing long dressing gown and towel on head.

If you see husband along the way, cover any exposed areas then sashay to the bedroom.

Take an hour and a half to get dressed.

HOW TO SHOWER LIKE A MAN

Take off clothes while sitting on the edge of the bed. Leave them in a pile on the floor.

Walk naked to the bathroom. If you see wife along the way, shake dick at her, making the "woo woo" sound.

Admire the size of your dick in the mirror and scratch your arse.

Get in the shower. Don't bother to look for a flannel because you don't use one.

Drizzle water on your face and hands.

Blow your nose in your hands.

Crack up at how loud your farts sound in the shower and then realise you shouldn't do it in a confined space.

Wash on your privates and surrounding area.

Wash your butt, leaving plenty of coarse hairs in the soap.

Shampoo hair, avoiding conditioner. Make a shampoo mohawk.

Rinse off and get out of the shower.

Fail to notice that you got water on the floor because you left the curtain hanging out of the tub.

Partially dry off.

Look at yourself in the mirror. Flex muscles. Admire the dick size again. Leave the shower curtain open and the wet bath mat on the floor.

Leave the bathroom fan and light on.

Return to the bedroom with the towel around your waist. If you pass wife, pull the towel off, shake your dick at her and make the "woo woo" sound again.

Throw the wet towel on the bed.

Take two minutes to throw on the clothes you were wearing before.

SNAPPIES

Two Eskimos sitting in a kayak were chilly, but when they lit a fire in the craft it sank – proving once and for all that you can't have your kayak and heat it.

Paul McCartney once bought his ex-wife Heather a plane for her birthday. She used hair remover on the other leg.

Maurice Gibb dies. Doctors say it was a TRAGEDY. He only had a NIGHT FEVER and they had every faith in him STAYING ALIVE.

An Essex girl is involved in a nasty car crash and is trapped and bleeding. The paramedics soon arrive on site. "It's OK I'm a paramedic and I'm going to ask you some questions?" "OK." "What's your name?" "Sharon." "OK Sharon, is this your car?" "Yes." "Where are you bleeding from?" "Romford, mate."

Two drunks are at a bar, drinking up a storm. One drunk says to the other drunk, "Did you sleep with my wife last night?" To which the other drunk replies, "Not a wink."

A man walks into a doctor's office. "What seems to be the problem?" asks the doc. "It's... um... well... I have five penises," replies the man. "Blimey!" says the doctor. "How do your trousers fit?" "Like a glove."

Two Irishmen on their first holiday to Florida are camping in the Everglades and they see an alligator with a guy's head and arms sticking out of its mouth. Paddy turns to Murphy and says, "Bejaysus Murphy, would you look at that flash bastard in the Lacoste sleeping bag!"

A couple is lying in bed. The man says, "I am going to make you the happiest woman in the world." The woman says, "I'll miss you."

"It's just too hot to wear clothes today," said Jack as he stepped out of the shower. "Honey, what do you think the neighbours would think if I mowed the lawn like this?" "Probably that I married you for your money," she replied.

BRIGHT LAD

A boy went up to his father and asked, "What is the difference between potentially and realistically?"

The father pondered for a while, then answered, "Go and ask your mother if she would sleep with Robert Redford for a million pounds. Also, ask your sister if she would sleep with Brad Pitt for a million pounds. Come back and tell me what you have learned."

So the boy went to his mother and asked, "Would you sleep with Robert Redford for a million pounds?"

The mother replied, "Of course I would. I wouldn't pass up an opportunity like that."

The boy then went to his sister and said, "Would you sleep with Brad Pitt for a million pounds?"

She replied, "Are you mad? I'd love to! I'd have to be insane not to, and damn Angelina!"

The boy then thought about it for a couple of days and went back to his father. His father asked, "Did you find out the difference between potentially and realistically?"

The boy replied, "Yes, potentially we're sitting on two million quid, but realistically we're living with a pair of slappers."

A LONG TIME COMING

A man and his wife are dining at a table in a plush restaurant, and the husband keeps staring at a drunken lady swigging her drink as she sits alone at a nearby table.

The wife asks, "Do you know her?"

"Yes," sighs the husband, "She's my ex-girlfriend. I understand she took to drinking right after we split up seven years ago, and I hear she hasn't been sober since."

"My God!" says the wife, "Who would think a person could go on celebrating that long?"!!

WOOF WOOF

Three Labrador retrievers - one brown, one black and one yellow were sitting in the vets' waiting room when they struck up a conversation. The black lab turned to the brown lab and said "So why are you here?"

The brown lab replied "I'm a p!sser. I p!ss on everything. The sofa, the curtains, the cat, the kids. But the final straw was last night when I p!ssed in the middle of my owners' bed."

The black lab said "So what is the vet going to do?"

"Going to cut my nuts off." replied the brown lab "They reckon it will calm me down."

The black lab turned to the yellow lab and said "Why are you here?"

The yellow lab said "I'm a digger. I dig under fences, dig up flowers and trees. I dig for the hell of it. When I'm inside, I dig up the carpets but I went over the line last night when I dug a great hole in my owners' couch." "So what are they going to do to you?" the black lab inquired. "Looks like I'm losing my nuts too" the dejected yellow lab said.

The yellow lab turned to the black lab and asked "Why are you here?" "I'm a humper" the black lab said "I'll hump anything. I'll hump the cat, the table, post boxes, whatever. I want to hump anything I see. Yesterday my owner had just got out of the shower and was bending down to dry her feet, and I just couldn't help myself.

I hopped on her back and started humping away".

The yellow and brown labs exchanged a sad glance and said "Nuts off for you too then huh?"

The black lab said "No — I'm here to get my nails clipped."

ALSO AVAILABLE IN ALL GOOD BOOKS STORES:

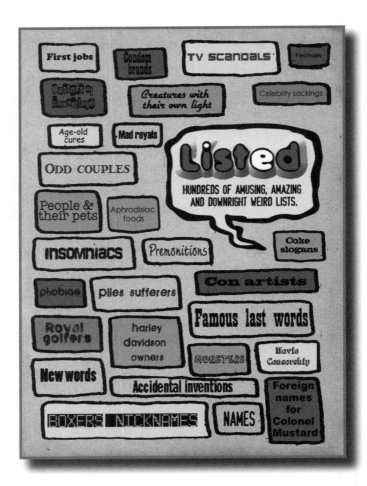